Voicing Power

VOICING POWER

CONVERSATIONS WITH VISIONARY WOMEN

edited by
Gail Hanlon

with a foreword by Gloria Steinem

WestviewPress
A Division of HarperCollins*Publishers*

Copyright © 1997 by Westview Press, A Division of HarperCollins Publishers, Inc.

Published in 1997 in the United States of America by Westview Press, 5500 Central Avenue, Boulder, Colorado 80301-2877, and in the United Kingdom by Westview Press, 12 Hid's Copse Road, Cumnor Hill, Oxford OX2 9JJ

Library of Congress Cataloging-in-Publication Data
Voicing power : conversations with visionary women / [edited by] Gail
   Hanlon ; with a foreword by Gloria Steinem.
      p.   cm.
   Includes bibliographical references.
   ISBN 0-8133-3203-6.—ISBN 0-8133-3204-4 (pbk.)
   1. Women social reformers—Interviews.   2. Feminism.   I. Hanlon,
Gail.
HN49.W6   1997
305.42—dc21   97-1291
                                                                                         CIP

Text design by Heather Hutchison

10   9   8   7   6   5   4   3   2   1

For Helena, with love

Contents

Foreword, Gloria Steinem   ix
Acknowledgments   xiii

    Introduction: *Gail Hanlon*   1

1   Living in a Liminal Time: *Jean Shinoda Bolen*   9

2   Radical Women: *Nancy Reiko Kato*   21

3   Homegrown Juju Dolls: *Riua Akinshegun*   33

4   Building Coalitions in the 1990s: *Flo Kennedy*   43

5   Supporting Our Frontline Struggles: *Winona LaDuke*   53

6   Children of All Nations: *Dhyani Ywahoo*   59

7   Creating a New Cultural Etiquette: *Amoja Three Rivers*   71

8   Healing Pain and Building Bridges: *Cherie Brown*   85

9   Meeting Us Halfway: *Carole Pope*   99

10   An Honorable Ethic: *Andrea Dworkin*   105

11   Defining Our Own Desires: *Deborah Anna Luepnitz*   123

12   Everyday Women's Values: *Karen Brodkin Sacks*   133

13   Envisioning a Partnership Future: *Riane Eisler*   143

14   Decolonizing Hearts and Minds: *Mililani B. Trask*   161

15   A Transformational Feminism: *Gerda Lerner*   177

16   Beyond Critique and Vision—Global Leadership
     in the Twenty-First Century: *Charlotte Bunch*   185

About the Book and Editor   199
List of Photo Credits   201

Foreword

GLORIA STEINEM

Any movement that cannot be sustained for fifty or a hundred years is not likely to accomplish its goal.

—*Gerda Lerner*

The female half of the world has a right to every form of expression, from music and poetry to storytelling and the novel. Indeed, we not only have the right to them, but the right to transform and redefine them to fit our experience. I remember my sense of revelation three decades ago when a feminist artist made me see that art itself had been defined politically. "'Art' is what men do in a European tradition," she explained. "'Crafts' are what women and natives do—but it's all the same thing."

In those days, we were also just realizing that our great musicians had been singing lullabies, our great sculptors making pottery, our great novelists writing in their diaries, and our great painters planting gardens. Though we were justifiably angry at the injustice this revealed, we soon realized that lullabies and pottery, diaries and gardens must also be included in the realm of art if all of human creativity was to be recognized. Even supposedly lesser forms of literature were soon being transformed in feminist hands. For example, feminists embraced science fiction, for they understood that its suspension of disbelief helped readers to imagine a world without the labels of sex or race, class or sexuality, and imagining change is the first step to achieving it. In a way, what feminists are talking about *is* science fiction.

For similar political reasons, the art of autobiography has been limited to those with the time, education, and ego to record their lives as well as to those with the support of the publishing world. Of course, women have always subverted such rules in our own sphere by sharing personal stories at the village well, exchanging wisdom at quilting bees, and daring to base an entire revolution on the political truths revealed in consciousness-raising groups. Nonetheless, we are only now beginning to do this in public, to claim crucial roles on the national and international stage, and to insist on the right of those at the periphery to transform the center. Just as democracy broadened the art of autobiography once restricted to nobles and leaders, liberation movements are widening this circle to include the female half of every class and race. After all, nothing can be complete—or completely understood—without everyone's story. As poet Muriel Rukeyser said, "The universe is made of stories, not atoms."

Woman of power magazine has always been important in widening the circle. It has given women a place to share their spirituality and thus to challenge many ways in which religion has been politics made sacred. It has created a safe place to discuss our very temporal differences, without fear that they will be used by those who oppose the goals we share. And its interviewers have asked serious questions, listened attentively, and generally bolstered our confidence that the wisdom gathered through female experiences deserves attention.

As you will see, Gail Hanlon and other editors of *woman of power* have encouraged diverse women to create an invaluable record. Some might never have taken time to share the wisdom of their work without these interviews, others might have lacked a sensitive listener who allowed them to speak as they would not do on paper, and still others might not have shared the many ways in which they are creating and redefining power and community. It may seem a long way from the nineteenth-century slave narrative to these interviews with contemporary workers in the feminist movement, but in both cases, unique and valuable women might otherwise never have recorded their experience at a particular time in history. Readers might have been robbed of a clear vision from the frontier of personal experience.

I have awaited every issue of *woman of power* in anticipation of exactly the kind of hard-earned wisdom that is now preserved in these pages. Each reader may take something different from *Voicing Power,* but each will find crucial knowledge for their lives and their work. To entice you onward, Gail Hanlon's introduction discusses many of the contributors. I will add a small sample of the insightful nuggets that live on for me.

From Amoja Three Rivers: "Sometimes I hear white women asking, 'How can we get more women of color to join our organization or come to our concerts?' I understand that they feel it's the right thing to do, but . . . we need to make things together, to start things up together, not start something and then ask someone else in after the fact."

From Cherie Brown: "Encourage people to tell their personal stories of discrimination and mistreatment. These stories are often emotional, and they touch people's hearts and open us up to our compassion. This is a very powerful way to assist women to see the pain and the struggle beneath the position with which they don't agree."

From Andrea Dworkin: "If prostitution had been empowering for women, we women would now be empowered."

From Carole Pope: "Ninety-eight percent of the women [prisoners] I work with are victims of incest, and 90 percent have been substance abusers for eleven years or more. They don't care about themselves. . . . The reality is that if you consistently show them that you care and keep giving them back their dignity and their humanity, many of them will begin to heal."

From Karen Brodkin Sacks: "Anybody who has to live in a subordinate group lives with two languages. You have to speak the boss's English, but your own experiences and socialization tell you that this is not a good language for you. You have a better one for yourself, but you have to be bilingual and bicultural."

From Deborah Anna Luepnitz: "Much of the longing for romance is a disguised desire for the sustaining power of community."

I would not want to pick only one form of expression as crucial to women, but if pressed to do so, it would be the telling of our personal stories. The vision that comes from day-to-day change is indispensable to sustaining our movement for the long term. Sharing our stories is the way we empower others—and honor ourselves. I hope you will add yours to the ones in this book.

Acknowledgments

A number of people contributed to the creation of this book. I owe special thanks to Charlene McKee, editor and cofounder of *woman of power* magazine, not only for sharing her knowledge and expertise but also for showing me the pleasure of working in collaboration. I would also like to thank Asoka Bandarage, guest editor of the issue on "Women of Color: A Celebration of Spirit" and Carolann Barrett for her editorial assistance at *woman of power.*

My sincerest thanks to the contributors who so generously gave of their time and whose eloquence made this book possible. I would also like to thank Helena Ragoné, my life partner, for her love, enthusiasm, and intellectual support. Although any shortcomings are, of course, my own, I would like to extend special thanks to Florence Boos, Sarah Franklin, and Jane Vanderbosch, whose comments greatly improved the introduction. I would also like to thank Gordon Massman, who originally accepted the manuscript for publication, and the editorial staff at Westview, especially Jill Rothenberg, Melanie Stafford, and Lisa Wigutoff.

Gail Hanlon

Voicing Power

Introduction

GAIL HANLON

———— • ◆ • ————

Politics, art, and the spiritual all have in common the power to envision, move and change. I like blurred boundaries.

—*Lucy Lippard*[1]

As the associate editor of *woman of power* magazine during the early 1990s, I was given a unique opportunity to interview some of the most engaging and visionary feminist activists, artists, and theorists now working in the United States and throughout the world. In this volume, sixteen of those interviews provide a selection of some of the most interesting and vital theory and activism now being generated as we approach the twenty-first century. *Voicing Power* traces several trajectories of thought concerning the meaning of global feminist leadership, with an emphasis on empowerment and positive spiritual, social, and cultural transformation.

From 1991 to 1995, the editorial staff of *woman of power* actively sought the contributions of women from diverse cultural and professional backgrounds in an effort to give voice to as many innovative and challenging perspectives as possible, particularly to points of view that were less well-represented in other forums. The women we sought held differing views of feminism, but all shared a deeply held sense of commitment to women's issues. The interview proved to be an ideal genre for our purposes, conveying as it did a sense of immediacy and the spontaneous, individual inflections sometimes lost in other written/textual forms and often erased from the historical record. Centered in the individual, the interview format allows us to hear each woman's voice—its pauses, refusals, and exclamations, how it trails off from or rewrites a classical plot. We experience each woman's language, her culture, and her vision, in her own time frame.

1

Reconnection and Reinvention

Perhaps one of the deepest sources of feminism's power is its potential to provide an integrative force, to restore a sense of profound and enduring interconnectedness to our lives. As I began to conduct interviews for the magazine, I found that it provided a kind of locus in which the intersecting but disparate issues of feminism, spirituality, and politics could be conjoined so as to "coalesce in their considerations of power."[2] Those intentionally "blurred boundaries," as Lucy Lippard calls them, graced us with a certain leeway to step outside of existing theoretical frameworks and political camps. It created a kind of clearing or crossroads, a place where a variety of eloquent, impassioned, and exciting voices could be heard.

It is, of course, often at the intersections of evolving and conflicting perspectives such as these that the most vital and fruitful changes are taking place in the women's movement, wherever the ferment of ideas refuses to settle into stasis. As someone who was profoundly interested in the intersection of feminism and spirituality but concerned about how it might be articulated and wary of dogma, I was delighted to find myself associated with so fine a forum for the exploration of these ideas. A subject somewhat difficult to access and often greatly distorted in Western culture, the contextualization of and foregrounding of spirituality (in conjunction with social action) proved to be of critical importance to these conversations. The magazine's statement of philosophy (created by a collective of women in the early 1980s) provided a clear and visionary background for many of the ideas that were emerging at that time. Although we rarely discussed "the sacred" per se, women's spirituality effectively rebraided into a single discourse these sometimes compartmentalized aspects of women's lives, providing a kind of clearing for the play of vision and critique. It also opened up or enlarged the field of conversation to suggest beauty, joy, and hope, those less tangible but essential needs, like the "roses" of "bread and roses" fame.[3]

Not surprisingly, the concept of "sanctuary," that elusive but critical ideal, emerged as a recurrent theme in these conversations. Jungian analyst Jean Shinoda Bolen, for example, describes the ideal therapeutic situation as one of *temenos* (the Greek term for "sanctuary"), a setting free of exploitation or judgement and herstorian Amoja Three Rivers celebrates her experience of various lesbian and women-of-color groups as one of sanctuary. Carole Pope describes her program for ex-convicts as a place to heal from the effects of sexual and physical abuse; Director of Sunray Meditation Center Dhyani Ywahoo outlines her plans to create "peace villages" for children in crisis; and activist Nancy Reiko Kato describes political struggle as a process through which "everyone is trying to create a sense of community . . . a safe space." At its best, the women's movement has provided sanctuary, and the challenge of living in the midst of a patriarchal culture while trying to envision, or repair, alternative forms of culture often provides another fruitful point of departure in these conversations. As author/activist Andrea Dworkin says from her perspective as a longtime participant in the women's movement, "the operative dynamic has to be empathy" for one another as we move away from "a world in which the dominant ethic is hierarchy and dominance."

Resources, Visions, and Values

As women around the world begin to reclaim their individual cultural traditions from the influence of patriarchal splintering, there is renewed hope that the "mythic underpinning of culture"[4] is shifting, producing the critical mass needed to create positive social change. The power of archetypal imagery and myth to influence behavior at the level of the subconscious, both positively and negatively, has yet to be fully articulated, but the contributions of the women artists, psychologists, theorists, spiritual leaders, and others in this collection are enlarging the scope of the collective feminist discourse.

The desire to restore meaningful connections in their lives—to reintegrate a range of resources, visions, and values—has led many women to the study of their own cultures, a process that often produces a profound shift in their worldview. Amoja Three Rivers, for example, who is of Native American and African descent, describes how her lifelong interest in history led to the study of traditional African cultures, where "spirituality is not separated out from . . . science or from the emotions. . . . Everything was interconnected, a single piece." Native American/African American Riua Akinshegun's artwork is also deeply influenced by the fusion of art and spirituality as practiced by contemporary Yoruba artists in Ife, Nigeria.

A number of women also discuss the history of their struggle to transform their work or profession into a vehicle for the integration of their feminist vision and values. Jean Shinoda Bolen, for example, who entered the profession of psychiatry at a time when the field had yet to be altered by a notion of patriarchy, defines psychology as a force for healing, its aim the integration of the individual psyche; and Nancy Reiko Kato outlines how she came to envision political action as a search for wholeness on an international scale. Lawyer/activist Flo Kennedy, an advocate for the inclusion of what she calls "the politics of your kids . . . the politics of your buying habits" in the feminist discourse, views her life's work as one of challenging false distinctions that relegate such issues to the realm of the "inconsequential."

Many of the women represented here attribute their strong personal sense of direction and desire for social justice to the inspiration of other women—from relatives in early childhood, to contemporary public figures such as Rigoberta Menchu, to historical figures such as Elizabeth Stone and spiritual images such as those of Amaterasu and the Virgin of Guadelupe. Mililani Trask, Native governor of Hawaii, for example, describes the empowering example set by her grandmother, a Native Hawaiian woman of "great heart and great integrity" who raised eight children and served as a respected community mediator. Systems theorist Riane Eisler recalls seeing her mother courageously challenge a group of Nazi soldiers, an early image that continues to serve as a powerful catalyst in her political life; and Anishinabe activist Winona LaDuke reveals how her social-justice work has been deeply influenced by the successes of other women such as the Innu activists who contested the construction of a NATO base in Labrador. Winona LaDuke and others celebrate the inspiration they receive from a growing global women's network, including the Indigenous Women's Network and the Mothers of East L.A., here in the United States; the Cordillera in the Philippines; the aboriginal women's movement in Australia; the Maori women's movement in New Zealand; and the African National Congress (ANC) and South African women's movement. (Having followed their itineraries via fax, E-mail, and telephone, I can attest to the international scope of the networking now taking place among women the world over.)

The restoration of these and other meaningful connections among feminist values and issues is also being powerfully translated into the realm of global policymaking and political theory. Charlotte Bunch, director of the Center for Women's Global Leadership, for example, proposes to see women's issues be placed at the heart of every human rights issue and made integral to every major political agenda, and historian Gerda Lerner emphasizes that the women's movement must be conjoined with other social justice movements if sufficiently complex, sustainable political alliances are to be forged.

Reconceptualizing Power; Reframing the Issues

Part of the feminist task has been to challenge false dichotomies, restoring vital points of connection between politics and spirituality (a distinction reified in theory but often violated in practice) and theory and practice, to the extent that they lessen our collective power. Identifying and healing existing conflicts while working to erase unnecessary dualisms—tracing out the implications of history; undertaking the careful, theoretical work; "converting knowledge to power";[5] and revitalizing language so that it accurately reflects women's realities—and, at the same time, remaining in touch with everyday concerns: These are the challenges of the movement as a whole and of the individual women interviewed here.

Each of the women represented in *Voicing Power* has her own personal and cultural relationship to the history of the women's movement—her own unique configuration of issues in which "women's issues" have played a greater or lesser part, depending on her life circumstances. From various backgrounds, the women in this collection also represent diverse paths of resistance to the diadic patterns in Western culture; each bridges various worlds so that her life is enriched and informed by her own culture and by the infusion of other ideas and practices.

As women establish needed links between theory and practice, the conceptual reframing of issues has also proved essential to clear communication within the women's movement. This is exemplified in the work of psychologist Deborah Anna Luepnitz, who analyzes the impact of personal healing on women's leadership, observing that "unconscious" as well as "conscious" motives often influence group processes. Cherie Brown, director of the National Coalition Building Institute, also emphasizes that "ongoing emotional healing work" is integral to sustained effective leadership.

Many of the women represented here were or are actively engaged in one or more related historical movements, such as the civil rights, Black power, antiwar, lesbian/gay rights, environmental, and indigenous movements. Each has her own *telos* or sense of purpose; her own experience of inclusion or exclusion, engagement or disengagement with the women's movement; and her own personal intellectual history of ideas formulated or rejected (so that, for example, the use of "criticism/self criticism" as a tool for the exploration of the intersection of personal and political in the 1970s elicits a range of responses).

Sustaining Vision and Encouraging Critique

At a time when feminism is at last beginning to take root, many of its ideas so well integrated as to be unrecognizable, the women represented in *Voicing Power* emphasize that the challenge of continuing to refine and redefine the vision of feminism for the future remains crucial. As Lerner reminds us, it took "seventy-two years of unremitting organization and struggle to secure the rights of suffrage. . . . Any movement that cannot be sustained for fifty or a hundred years is not likely to accomplish its goal." Perhaps one of the best indications of feminism's resilience and vitality is exhibited in its refusal to settle into a single, fixed system or paradigm; in this sense, it remains a vital site in constant flux, one that continues to avail itself of new and salutory trajectories.

With its various and seemingly contradictory opinions, methods, and strategies, *Voicing Power* illustrates how it is that very different visions can coexist through the passionate and unrelenting commitment to improve the quality of women's lives, with feminism as the rubric, however provisional, for this essential work. The voices in this collection represent the confluence of a number of branches of feminism, reflecting the women's movement's diversity and continued growth as a force for the implementation of what anthropologist Karen Brodkin Sacks has called "a vision of just and humane social relations." In these conversations, we are reminded that various changes (many of them, such as the "critical interrogation of the universal category 'woman,'"[6] instituted by marginalized women) have allowed the movement to develop in a number of new directions while retaining as its essential goal the liberation of all women (and others) through compassionate action.

As women whose issues have been regrettably marginalized by the movement continue to challenge its assumptions from within, transforming its aims with new and vital visions, the movement has become increasingly self-reflexive, its understandings reinvigorated and increasingly multidimensional. These changes have, as bell hooks says, "strengthened the power of feminist thought . . . [and] compelled feminist thinkers to problematize and theorize issues of solidarity."[7] Because "you cannot sweep a room without stirring up the dust,"[8] sustaining and developing these understandings will entail a willingness to seek out "areas of common view," as Dhyani Ywahoo calls them, points of reference in the collective struggle to "create the field of justice." As the many voices of the women in this volume remind us, great care must be taken to remember that what is sought is marginalized knowledge, that which concerns itself with a "historical knowledge of struggle,"[9] especially now as women's issues begin to approach the center of other discourses.

Perhaps the most difficult to identify but most essential contributions of feminism are those aspects that represent lived experience, especially if we consider feminism a "pilgrimage" of the kind described by Jean Shinoda Bolen, a process in which "changes are effected on other than a cognitive, abstract, verbal level." It is my hope that *Voicing Power* will preserve some of the vitality invariably lost when the historical record smooths over the conflicting, vibrant details of how each wave of women's history (and other histories) was experienced by those who lived it.

As I wrote in the introduction to the "Leadership" issue in the summer of 1995, women have only begun to outline the many ways in which feminism is being developed and transformed as the twentieth century comes to a close. We live in an exciting intellectual period in which many of the early premises of feminism are being challenged, many of its truths are being implemented, and many of its goals are becoming more sophisticated, diffuse, and multiform. The language with which to describe women's experience is being developed, the "lost sources of knowledge and of spiritual vitality"[10] recovered, the conceptual frameworks perfected and in some cases razed, and "new tools for personal and collective empowerment"[11] defined. Informed by a history of debate and by the contributions of other discourses, there is reason to hope that a feminist leadership that is rooted increasingly in social activism and tempered by theory, renewed by an openness of spirit, and no longer considered invariable across traditions and domains will provide vision and direction as women continue to transform their societies.

Notes

1. *The Pink Glass Swan: Selected Essays on Feminist Art*, Introduction: "Moving Targets/Concentric Circles: Notes from the Radical Whirlwind" (New York: New Press, 1995), p. 10.

2. "Statement of Philosophy," *woman of power* magazine.

3. "We want bread and roses too" (the organizing slogan of women strikers in Lawrence, MA, in 1912).

4. Jean Shinoda Bolen, "Women of Color: A Celebration of Spirit," *woman of power* Issue #21, p. 22.

5. Adrienne Rich, *Lies, Secrets, and Silence: Selected Prose 1966–1978*, "Toward a Woman-Centered University" (New York: Norton, 1979), p. 128.

6. Bell hooks, *Outlaw Culture: Resisting Representations* (New York: Routledge, 1994), p. 102.

7. Bell hooks, *Outlaw Culture*, p. 102.

8. A traditional African saying, quoted by Amoja Three Rivers, "Women in Community," *woman of power* Issue #22, p. 11.

9. Nicholas B. Dirks, Geoff Eley, and Sherry B. Ortner, eds., *Culture/Power/History: A Reader in Contemporary Social Theory* (Princeton, NJ: Princeton University Press, 1994), p. 203.

10. Rich, *Lies, Secrets, and Silence*, p. 126.

11. "Statement of Philosophy," *woman of power* magazine.

1

Living in a Liminal Time

JEAN SHINODA BOLEN

Jean Shinoda Bolen, M.D., is a psychiatrist and Jungian analyst in private practice. She is the author of *Goddesses in Everywoman, The Tao of Psychology, Crossing to Avalon, Close to the Bone: Life-Threatening Illness and the Meaning of Life,* and other books, and is an internationally known lecturer.

A clinical professor of psychiatry at the University of California Medical School and a former member of the Ms. Foundation, she has long been an advocate for women's issues and ethics in psychiatry. Bolen is also a Fellow of the American Psychiatric Association, a Diplomate of the American Board of Psychiatry and Neurology, and a Fellow of the American Academy of Psychoanalysis. She founded and cochaired Psychiatrists for ERA, a major influence within psychiatry in the early 1980s, which evolved into the Association for Women in Psychiatry. She is also a board member of the International Transpersonal Association.

All of Bolen's work places an emphasis on the quest for meaning and the need for a spiritual dimension in our lives, taking into account the powerful effects of archetypes, the family, and culture. Her grandparents

9

on both sides came to the United States from Japan after having converted to Christianity. "Metaphors such as 'straddling two worlds' or having binocular vision," Bolen says, "describe the perspective from which my perceptions come. It is a way of seeing and being in the world that grows out of being 'other' and yet 'accepted' in my many worlds . . . the way it is for many women of color."

Bolen also appears in two widely acclaimed documentaries, "Goddess Remembered," the first of the Canadian Film Board's trilogy on women's spirituality, and the Academy Award–winning antinuclear documentary "Women: For America, For the World." She lives in northern California, practices in San Francisco, and has a son and daughter.

woman of power: How would you describe the work you are currently doing?

Jean Shinoda Bolen: My work is in three parts these days: my clinical practice as a Jungian analyst, my writing, and the lectures and workshops that I present. All of them have to do with empowering or inspiring people to determine for themselves what matters to them; they learn not to give that power over to somebody else, whether it be the family or the patriarchal culture. When I first entered the profession of psychiatry, we really didn't have a notion of patriarchy. The whole notion that we were defined and limited by stereotypes came with the women's movement. And then by bridging the worlds of the women's movement and Jungian psychology, I could see that women, since I was at that point in my writing focusing on women, were greatly shaped by the archetypes inside of us as well as the stereotypes outside of us. Consciousness raising required that we be aware of both. Then women who were reading *Goddesses in Everywoman* began to use it as a text on women's spirituality, although it had started out as a psychology of women.

woman of power: Do you think that under ideal circumstances clinical psychology could be considered a form of spiritual practice?

Bolen: Yes. First of all, my work comes out of a strong heart place and a sense that each of us has a strong spiritual center. One needs to remember that the word for psychology, *psyche* in Greek, means "soul" or "butterfly." Thus, it really is about soul growth and transformation. I think that most clinical psychologists at their best are responding to a wish to heal their patients, and that each school of thought has its own focus as to what is the cause of the suffering or the wounding that leads to the symptoms, and that each provides a different method to help. But most of them leave out the soul or the spiritual dimension, except in Jungian psychology and transpersonal psychology. We also have the twelve-step programs, which really could be considered a psychology, and which were from the very beginning influenced by Jung and carried as their charge the idea that the healing will come as the individual with the addiction gets in touch with the Self.

woman of power: What do you see happening in the women's spirituality movement?

Bolen: I see women's spirituality as a quiet, gradual movement all over this country and in other countries as well. When the concepts are introduced, women respond because words are being given to something that they intrinsically seem to know. I feel that it is being ignored by the greater culture because it doesn't claim any turf. It is not competitive for the power that exists in the outer world. It is an interior, empowering movement that was being ignored until the concept of the Goddess became more widespread. In recent years the media has begun to write features on the Goddess movement. But what they seem to be drawn to is just the tip of the iceberg. Although women's spirituality is about the Goddess, many women wouldn't even say it is so, because "the Goddess" has many different, individual forms of expression.

I think that women's spirituality has to do with recognizing that there is a sacred dimension to the feminine, which therefore has an enormous number of definitions. But when a woman feels that there is something sacred in her life, in herself, which is related to the feminine aspect of herself and the embodiment of a divine quality in the Earth, in nature, in other human beings, it is a quiet spirituality. It doesn't require institutions; it doesn't require dogma. This interior knowing is what always interests me in my work, giving individuals a sense that they are the authority in their own lives and that they should not give to others the power to label, or define, what is significant and deeply human to them. I think all of this work is saying much the same thing, that we are basically on a spiritual path, and that the choices we make in life matter. Those choices are based on consciousness and following what only we can know is deeply meaningful and it is based on love.

woman of power: Can you talk about how those individual choices transform culture as a whole?

Bolen: Well, it begins with an individual's quest for truth and freedom. It begins in the simple form with which the women's movement first began, which was the circle, within which one told the truth of one's own life. That was empowering, not only for the woman who spoke her truth but also for the women who heard it and were then inspired or empowered to do the same. In good psychotherapy that also happens: there is a safe place. I call it—and others do too, but I specifically refer to it as—a *temenos,*[1] which is Greek for sanctuary. Within that sanctuary, it is understood that one will not be exploited or judged. Whatever is said about what one has done, what one feels, or what one aspires to is received as if in a sanctuary. Then whatever is said gradually becomes more true.

The latest movement in psychology has to do with the awareness that twelve-step programs have brought to us and out of that comes the notion that the great majority of us come from dysfunctional families. The number is very large because we live in a dysfunctional society. If you're in a dysfunctional society—that is, a patriarchy within which power is the ruling principle—then truth suffers because telling the truth is not always safe. Consequently, in order to keep yourself safe, you repress what you know to be true because it is dangerous to speak it. And gradually you become inarticulate, and then perhaps numb to what it is you fear and what it is you know to be true, until you find yourself in a safe place, or *temenos,* where you can gradually acknowledge what is true.

So whether it be a women's group, or a twelve-step group, or a safe psychotherapy relationship, or, where it often happens among women, in friendships that have extended over years, there has to be a safe place where we can tell the truth if we are to remember, perceive, feel, and know what is true. The authenticity that results is a challenge to the established order, which is hierarchical and patriarchal and based on power. So as individuals first know the truth and then speak it, the greatest potential lies in the transformation that happens within individual relationships, where one person starts telling the truth and it affects the system. This process may begin with a couple, a family, or an institution. If people were in circles of truth, then it would certainly be a different kind of culture, where people wouldn't put on a persona or a false face and would be willing to be vulnerable and to tell the truth. Of course, women are better at that than men, so we will do it first.

woman of power: Do you think that healing is taking place on a mythic level in the sense that cultural stereotypes are being transformed by the women's movement?

Bolen: I think that we are in the midst of a transformative myth right now, one having to do with the emergence of the Goddess into individual psyches and the return of the Goddess into the culture. In a culture that is patriarchal in its religion, everything that is feminine and of women is degraded, held to be inferior, and not of divinity. We have a Judeo-Christian tradition that says that men are created in the image of God and are here to have dominion over everything, especially over that which is considered of the feminine. The whole point of the hierarchy is that everything closest to God is always represented as male. Also, patriarchal culture defines some things as masculine and others as feminine and considers the latter inferior. So these qualities, which are in truth in everyone regardless of gender, are repressed or devalued in everyone.

When divinity carries a feminine face, and when there is reverence for that divinity, the mythic underpinning of culture as we know it shifts greatly, because then we no longer have a dominator culture that has power over an inferior culture. If the culture has a return of the experience of the feminine as divinity, the Earth as having a sacred dimension, and if women are considered to be in the image of the Goddess, that is, carriers of life who bring through their bodies the miracle of birth, then those very things that are considered animalistic by masculine spiritual standards become holy. And you treat that which is holy differently. So if the Goddess is coming back, as I truly feel She is, as an archetypal underpinning for healing experiences, there would be a major shift in how the Earth and women and the feminine are treated. That would be a major revolution. Actually I think of it more as an evolution.

woman of power: What do you think remains to be done if this evolution of the Goddess is to take place?

Bolen: Enough individuals have to evolve, however many it takes to become a critical mass, until what was once unthinkable becomes the norm. For example, for about twenty years after atomic bombs were dropped on Hiroshima and Nagasaki in 1945, everybody to some extent was aware that the potential to destroy the Earth existed. Because of the Cold War and the developing stockpiles of these weapons, it was assumed that there was nothing we could do about the inevitability of it. We felt powerless.

But somewhere along the line, individuals started to break through that numbing. An empowering myth that helped to sustain people who toiled at what others thought of as an impossible task was the story of The Hundredth Monkey, which was tied into the notion of the morphic field, introduced by Rupert Sheldrake, a theoretical biologist. He theorized that when a critical number is reached, the behavior or thinking of that entire species shifts. The Hundredth Monkey story is based on the idea that for society to change, someone has to be the first monkey, and someone has to be the fourteenth, and someone has to be the seventy-ninth, for there to be "a hundredth monkey"—whoever it is that tips the scales and, by so doing, changes the thinking of humanity.

I think that that is what happened in the nuclear situation. And although we still have nuclear weapons capabilities, something has shifted in the behavior of the major powers and in consciousness in general, and nuclear war is no longer considered an inevitability.

Each of us who perceives the feminine aspect of divinity, Mother God, the Goddess, however it is that we experience divinity as female, or as also female, is contributing to the resacralization of the Earth and women, and at the same time is influencing a morphic field that has to do with the return of the Goddess into the culture. Major cultural shifts can happen within a couple of hundred years. We now know that there was once a matriarchal culture; we certainly know that it was replaced by a patriarchal culture. As we move out of this second millennium into the third millennium we are, archetypally, entering into a critical passage time, when change can happen. We're approaching that critical transition now. It is what I call a liminal time, a time between worlds, between old and new; "liminal" refers to the threshold or doorway of a place as well as a time of transition. The integration of the sacred dimension of the feminine is a major element in this transition.

Yet every transition time is fraught with the potential for transformation and the potential for destruction. There can be resistance to change because forces of repression can be activated. Look at what happened in China to the students in Tiananmen Square for whom the Goddess of Democracy was a major symbol, or at efforts to reverse the Supreme Court's *Roe v. Wade* decision.

woman of power: With respect to moving beyond patriarchal or Graeco-Roman archetypes do you think that everything is available to us at that archetypal level?

Bolen: We have within us the potential to access the patterns that have preceded us, just as in our bodies there are remnants of the evolution that we've made. So we have gills in our necks that are literally covered over, but sometimes they're not covered over completely so that there are cysts in the neck that come from the gill space. Just as the body has recollections of the evolution, so does the psyche. We share a collective unconscious, which means that we have access to the thought patterns of life that preceded us, but we also have the potential to evolve new patterns.

That whole notion of morphic fields that I mentioned earlier provides the theory that would explain how archetypes can also come into being and evolve in us. I definitely do not believe that all we have is what we used to have and forgot. Life itself has transformational potential built into it, why should this be different? Why should we be limited in our minds so that all we can tap into is what has gone on before?

woman of power: What do you envision for feminism in the 1990s?

Bolen: I think that the spiritual dimension is the last and the most significant wave of the women's movement, and that once the model of divinity having a feminine face is brought into the culture, the culture can change. It seems to me that that is in process. I see us generating new archetypes and cultural myths, with the image of Earth from outer space perhaps the most significant new symbol. The Earth is Mother, Gaia, matter, an icon that evokes emotion and imagination. As boundaries and borders diminish and disappear, significance is taken away from artificial, tangible barriers like the Berlin Wall or ideological ones like the Iron Curtain. They lose archetypal significance, and the power of the collective to uphold them as walls lessens until they come down. The image of Earth from outer space also evokes an enlargement of the archetype of Home, which in turn enlarges the notion of hearthkeeping and caretaking. Children of the Earth are growing into maturity and taking on responsibilities. Divinity is increasingly perceived as both Mother and Father. I'm encouraged by all of this, as I think it points in the direction of evolutionary change.

woman of power: What do you envision for women of color in the 1990s?

Bolen: There is a connection between the oppression, exploitation, and devaluation of women and people of color, the ecological rape of the Earth, and the absence of an Earth Mother spirituality. With a return of the Goddess in her many and varied aspects, psychological values will shift, and this will have enormous positive consequences for the Earth and for women—especially women of color. When god is disembodied—thought of as a powerful, white, male, sky god—the person most "other" is female, of color, and in her body. When there are female images of divinity, there is diversity and particularity. This was characteristic of Goddess spirituality in past historical times as it is now in the emerging Goddess movement. There are dark- and light-skinned images of the Goddess, and maiden, mother, or crone figures, with European, Asian, or African features.

When any female child anywhere can find qualities in herself mirrored back to her by an image of the Goddess, then her positive sense of herself is enhanced, and when others see the Goddess in her as well, it will affect how she is treated and valued. So it is with the Earth, if it is related to as Gaia or Mother Earth or Home, then it—She—will be cared for.

What has been lacking in the mythology of western civilization is a loving and powerful mother. All the mythologies are about powerless women. But when you grow up in a family where your mother is a strong and competent human being, you get a different experience of what the feminine is. All children should have a direct experience of having strong, competent women for mothers.

The values of western civilization whose roots are Greek and Judeo-Christian have set the standards for the rest of the world which the West colonized and made into a market for its products and ideas. That which is "earthy" or dark in color, female, instinctual, natural, or physical in expression is repressed, considered inferior, dangerous, and in need of control or punishment—making it "all right" to be abusive toward people so perceived. Women of color then become the recipient of "dark" projections—forbidden passions and yearnings for earthy experience, for fulfillment of dependency needs. Intelligence is not ascribed to people who are darker or female in the Third World when the so-called First World makes this an attribute of individuals who are white and male.

The power to define, name, and have dominion over others is exercised by patriarchy, with devastating consequences to those who become labelled inferior and treated as such, as well as to the Earth and all life upon it. In a desacralized, soulless, Goddessless world, everything that exists is exploited rather than cared for, because there is no spiritual reason to treat the material world with respect, love, or stewardship. "Matter," "material," and "matrix" have the same linguistic roots as "mother" and "maternal"; when humanity experiences the material world as partaking in the immanent divinity of the feminine, there will be a paradigm shift that changes perception and behavior.

woman of power: How does your work as a Jungian analyst relate to this?

Bolen: In the dreams that I hear in my office and that are shared with me as I travel and lecture, Goddess figures frequently appear or speak to the dreamer. These dreams stand out because they are usually numinous—meaning that there is a felt quality of awe and significance in the encounter. The dream figure makes a profound impression; in the telling it is as if "she" is a capitalized "She." Often she is a large dark-skinned woman and there is a Goddess quality about her presence. Marion Woodman's comments in an interview first made me aware that what I was hearing was a transpersonal phenomenon. "For some time now," she said, "I have been hearing dreams—hundreds of dreams from both sexes—about big dark women. These . . . women are a redeeming symbol because they have contact with the body and a love for it."[2] In order for there to be the emergence of a major new archetype or the return of a repressed one into the culture, I would expect that image to appear in the dreams and art of individuals, and this is happening.

A large, dark woman is the very opposite of the standard of beauty and femininity that we see reflected all around us, where already-slender Caucasian models have their curves airbrushed out. When such images are the standard, the inability to look like this is a source of self-hatred for women who are darker and have fuller figures and ethnic features. Powerful dream experiences are real events in that they do impact upon the psyche of the dreamer and can change the attitude of the dreamer. To encounter an awesome Goddess figure in a dream is a personal and authentic experience; awakening and seeing other women or oneself as a reflection of this figure has an effect as a positive revaluation on what had been previously devalued.

We can draw our own conclusions when we have such an experience, not just in dreams but in life or even through television. For example, to see Barbara Jordan during the televised Watergate hearings was to experience beauty and intelligence and presence in a large Black woman. I wonder how many young Black women gained a role model as a result and thus became empowered with the realization that it would be wonderful to grow up to look or be like her?

Goddess spirituality has an enormous potential to affect individual psychology as well as cultural values. In this time of transition, individuals are changing—and each of us who does change brings the possibility of a shift in a cultural paradigm closer.

woman of power: Was there anything else you wanted to say about the theme of the issue, "Women of Color: A Celebration of Spirit"?

Bolen: I would like us to link at the archetypal level with all women at the same time that we feel the uniqueness and richness of our particular ethnicity, appearance, or traditions. One of the things I see in women's spirituality is a connection that many women have to their own cultural archetypes. For example, the chief divinity in Japanese culture is the Goddess Amaterasu. In every culture that I know of, the embodiment of the wisdom that was repressed is considered feminine. I think it is possible to hold within our psyches an awareness of having a feminine identity that is both universal and unique at the same time. By being born female and inhabiting a woman's body, we share an experience with all women throughout time and throughout the world; and because of the particulars of skin color, social class, family, country and historical time, we are also in distinct and separate groups.

I know that if there is a return of the Goddess she will have many names, faces, and manifestations, and individual women will feel her presence within themselves. In my mind's eye, I see a circle of women of many races, of all ages and situations, each having a sense of herself as an extension of the Goddess, and each thus having the expectation that she will be treated with respect. By acting from this premise, these women—my sisters—can change the world. It is fitting that we say *"Namaste"* to one another in turn, by which we mean, "the Goddess in me beholds and honors the Goddess in you."

woman of power: Do you think that therapy and spirituality can be considered as forms of consciousness raising for women?

Bolen: I think that they can be tremendously empowering. When I was on the board of the Ms. Foundation for Women, one of the things I could see was that if women's centers attended to a spiritual source, they would nurture women, inspire them, and help them to endure. It is very difficult to stand on the front lines with only outrage to sustain us. In order to sustain ourselves on the front lines, I think we really have to tap into something that truly nurtures us. Part of what nurtures us is working in the company of other women, which is clearly one of the major nurturing presences. But beyond that, there is a deeper need to be in touch with what could be called the archetype of the Self. In order to have a sense that at some really deep level this is sacred work, we need to feel the empowerment of the archetype itself as we do the work. So I think the most effective warriors need to be in touch with the archetypal Self so that there is compassion as well as anger. There is a whole other level of changing the world that involves compassionate action as well as outrage in action. Outrage may begin it; but somewhere along the line, if the shift can be made to sustain that forward movement through the spiritual dimension, it will be greatly enriched.

woman of power: What is the source of your spirit or your energy? What empowers you personally?

Bolen: When I was a teenager, I had a direct sense of God so that I did not end up questioning that there is a soul element. And then as my life progressed, that spiritual dimension continued to be a part of my life but it took different forms. I had a sense that women share a truly sacred dimension by being able to carry a new life into this world, through direct expression and experience. It was actually in childbirth, during labor and delivery, that I joined the women's movement. Before then I somehow didn't see the issues as particularly mine, but that particular experience made me aware not only of the sacred dimension of what we experience being in a woman's body, it also gave me tremendous respect for and a sense of connection with every woman who had ever given birth.

And thank goodness for all the women who wrote all the feminist anthologies in the seventies. When I gave birth to my first child, all that information was available to me along with the perspective that I had gained from working with women patients. It was a combination of all of this that brought me into the women's movement. I also felt more like Artemis than any of the other Goddesses. Archetypally, Artemis is the sister, the woman who has a woman-to-herself quality, so that, too, was part of the archetypal and spiritual underpinnings that contributed to my entering the women's movement.

And then there was my own evolution through pilgrimages to sacred places on the Earth. It is said that pilgrims go on pilgrimage to "quicken the divinity," and experience something that they couldn't experience by staying at home. I could feel in my body the energy of places that had been sacred to the Goddess, the druids, and the Christians, and that was a turning point for me. It changed me and the changes were effected on other than a cognitive, abstract, verbal level. This experience told me something about my connection on a sacred level with the Earth, that my body and the Earth were in communion at some level.

It is empowering to have the experience of knowing something deeply, regardless of whether you can explain it to anyone else. Most people have had such an experience, and many of them don't place value on it, and therefore it doesn't instruct their lives. What a mistake this is! All my work really has to do with helping people to remember and reconnect with their own sources of union with divinity and meaning, because I know firsthand that creativity, authenticity, and depth grow out of this.

Notes

1. *Temenos* is described more fully in *Ring of Power*, by Jean Shinoda Bolen, (New York: HarperCollins, 1992).

2. See Marion Woodman, *The Tarrytown Letter*, published by the Tarrytown Group, No. 54, December 1985/January 1986.

References

Bolen, Jean Shinoda. "From Penis Envy to Goddesses in Everywoman: Revising Theory to Fit Experience." *Women & Therapy Journal*, Vol. 11:1 (1991).

Bolen, Jean Shinoda. *The Wisewoman Archetype: Menopause as Initiation.* (Boulder, CO: Sounds True Audiotape, 1991).

Bolen, Jean Shinoda. *Goddesses in Everywoman.* (San Francisco: Harper & Row, 1984).

Keyes, Jr., Ken. *The Hundredth Monkey.* (Coos Bay, OR: Vision Books, 1982).

Schaef, Anne Wilson. *Women's Reality: An Emerging Female System in a White Male Society.* (San Francisco: Harper & Row, 1981); and *When Society Becomes an Addict.* (San Francisco: Harper & Row, 1987).

Sheldrake, Rupert. *A New Science of Life: The Hypothesis of Formative Causation.* (Los Angeles: Tarcher, 1981); and "Mind, Memory, and Archetype: Morphic Resonance and the Collective Unconscious," *Psychological Perspectives* (published by the C. G. Jung Institute, Los Angeles) Vol. 18:1 (1987).

Woodman, Marion. *The Pregnant Virgin.* (Toronto: Inner City Books, 1985).

2

Radical Women

NANCY REIKO KATO

Nancy Reiko Kato is the organizer of Bay Area Radical Women and is on the National Executive Committee of Radical Women. A *sansei*, or third generation Japanese American, Kato was raised in Albany, a small town near Berkeley, California. She learned activism very early on when her mother encouraged her involvement in community issues through the Berkeley Buddhist Temple. Her mother also took her to the International Hotel in San Francisco, site of the last remaining building in what had been known as Manila Town, home to the city's Filipino population. In 1968, when the hotel's owners tried to evict the tenants in order to replace the building with a parking lot, a nine-year struggle ensued.

As an ethnic studies major at the University of California at Berkeley, Kato became a core member of the defense committee for Merle Woo, who had lost her teaching position because of her support for efforts to retain community-based lecturers, language courses, and student input in the Asian American Studies department. When a union grievance was filed, Woo was rehired—a victory that inspired Kato to go on to work as an organizer for Radical Women, an international feminist organization founded in 1967 that now has offices in the United States, Canada, and Australia. She is a trade-union activist in the American Federation of

State, County, and Municipal Employees, a campus rabble-rouser, an editor for the law journal at UC Berkeley, an antifascist organizer, and a defender of reproductive rights. Kato is also the author of *Women of Color: Frontrunners for Freedom,* a pamphlet that provides a theoretical perspective on the leadership of women of color. Articles about Kato's work have appeared in *The International Examiner* and *Northwest Nikkei.*

———————•◆•———————

Author's note: Radical Women is a multiracial, socialist feminist organization that works to foster the leadership of women. We are both activists and theoreticians, committed to working in coalition with other groups and individuals regarding common issues. Founded in 1967, Radical Women is an international organization that is the left wing of the feminist movement and the feminist wing of the radical movement. Radical Women believes that women of color and poor and working-class women will provide the leadership for feminism's third wave in the 1990s, unlike feminism's first wave, the suffragist movement, and the second wave, the women's movement of the 1960s. We believe that women, particularly women of color, will provide the leadership that is necessary to usher in the revolutionary change for which the majority of the world's people struggle. We believe that women of color, who face daily sexism, racism, and job discrimination, will lead militant movements because they have the least to lose and the most to gain from the end of capitalism.

woman of power: *Will you elaborate on your statement that "Radical change— as in going to the root or source—ain't gonna happen without women of color at the very center of the struggle, teaching, administering, coordinating, inspiring, speaking, and drawing the movements together"?*[1]

Nancy Reiko Kato: By radical change, I mean that we have to get to the source of our problems. I believe that the source of our problems—homelessness, lack of education, major budget crises, racism, sexism, homophobia, all the "isms"—is the capitalist system under which we live. As things get worse, people don't even have the basics anymore. They are fighting among themselves for necessities, and I don't believe that this system can give these things to them, because if it could, it would. Many people are beginning to understand that the society in which we live cannot provide for them anymore, and what they want is an alternative—a radical, revolutionary alternative.

I think that women of color have always been at the center of any radical change, we're just not recognized as such. For example, in the civil rights movement, Black women were really some of the more militant participants in the struggle. From our perspective, women of color see the interconnectedness of race, of sex, of class, and of sexuality. One of the reasons I am an activist is that I want to bring all those different parts of myself together. I think women of color understand that. We see that we want to be whole people and that the society we live in chops us up into little pieces and abuses us because of it. Women of color naturally integrate the issues of race and sex and class together because we experience all of these. I think that women of color will be at the center of the struggle because what keeps people from working together in this day and age are differences based on race, sex, sexuality, and class. And because we want to integrate all those groupings together, our role is to bring everything together and we do that from our own experiences.

I know that when I am discriminated against it is not just because of sexism, or just because of racism, it is because of both things. I understand that those things keep us divided from our natural allies and I understand that we need to work beyond such divisions. It is in my own best interest to reach out to, for instance, white women or men of color so that we can work together regarding common issues.

Women of color are already there, at the center of every social justice movement, but we have to be very firm about fighting for all of our issues. So if, for example, in the reproductive rights movement, feminists are saying that they just want to make abortion legal without talking about full reproductive rights, women of color will make those connections and insist upon them. The National Organization for Women is working to "save abortion rights," without understanding and recognizing that abortion has been unavailable for many poor women and women of color since the Hyde Amendment. Women of color are saying, "Yes, let's talk about abortion rights, but let's also talk about sterilization abuse. Let's also talk about parental consent. Let's also talk about prenatal care." If you don't take up all the issues that are interconnected at once, you're going to have a very segmented and segregated movement, because women of color are not going to put their energies into a movement that stresses only one aspect of their lives.

woman of power: What changes do you see ahead for feminism in the 1990's?

Kato: I think feminism is becoming a lot more radical. Many feminists today are not satisfied with identity politics, personal solutions, or blaming men as the source of our problems. They are tired of merely hearing about the problems because they already know firsthand what they are. People want solutions and they're willing to act on those solutions, to take action in order to implement them. Once again, given the economic times in which we live, I think that the feminist movement as a whole and all the movements for social change are going to be forced to be more radical, and more demanding. They will be forced to say, "We need this, we want this, and you had better give it to us." I think that that is really very exciting. We really have nothing to lose. If you don't have a job, or you don't have a home, or your kids don't have an education, then you don't have a lot to lose when you demand something from the government.

I think that the core of any social movement, or forward movement, is leadership. If you don't have effective leaders, educating and advocating certain types of actions, then people either won't do anything, or they'll be distracted from keeping their eyes on the prize. We fight hard for things. We fight very hard for different types of forums, whether it is lesbian and gay rights, or reproductive rights, or civil rights, and we've seen how easily they are taken away, for example, in recent Supreme Court decisions. So now I think people understand that while we need to fight for reforms and legislation and laws, we've also got to fight for more than that. The laws are in the hands of the government and it has shown over the years that it doesn't work in our interest at all.

woman of power: When you say that people want more radical change, what exactly do you mean? What kinds of trends have you seen?

Kato: In response to the budget crisis in California, a recent poll indicated that people were saying, "Tax the rich, make them pay their fair share." That is getting to the heart of the problem, people understanding who is benefiting from the budget crunch and who is not—why we don't have enough money to begin with. I think that is fairly radical. It is making demands on the system and recognizing that the government is a problem, that the political system we live under is a problem.

woman of power: How do you envision women of color, poor women, and working-class women providing leadership for feminism in the next decade?

Kato: I see them stepping forward as leaders because if you're pushed into a corner, the only way out is to fight. I believe that people want to make things better for themselves, so they'll fight to do that. Sometimes it takes them a long time to get to that point. It takes a lot of different things to get people to stand up. But I believe that, generally speaking, people do stand up. When things hit you on a very personal level, you realize that you'd better act to stop something bad from happening, like losing your job, or losing your house, or not having an education for your children. You're going to take a stand.

I see that a lot these days. People are beginning to understand that they can't wait until they lose their jobs. They can't wait until the schools shut down to do something. Once again, it is poor women and women of color who are being hit the hardest. They're talking about cutting Aid to Families with Dependent Children to save money, yet these women live below the poverty line already. The ones who are hit the hardest are the ones who are going to be on the front lines.

woman of power: Do you think that this trend will continue if things improve economically in the 1990s?

Kato: I don't think it is going to get better in the 1990s. Capitalism's whole purpose is to expand profit, and it is not able to do that because there are no more markets left to tap. In the 1990s, I think we'll see a showdown. We're at a historical crossroads in that capitalism is in decline; it is almost dead, and it is going to increase its exploitation of us and intensify its attacks on us in order to survive.

So I think that the 1990s will be a very exciting time. They may be a very hard time, a terrible time even, but I have a lot of optimism and faith that people will rise to the occasion and will rise up against the government, big business, and the state, and say, "We don't want to live like this anymore." They're willing to build a better world. I think that socialism is an alternative that people are willing to examine more closely, because a system based on equality is what is needed.

woman of power: How do you respond to the claim that socialism is a utopian idea?

Kato: There are a couple of ways I respond to that. One is that if people are saying it is utopian based on what is happening in Eastern Europe, or the Soviet Union, or even Cuba, I don't believe that those are really socialist countries. I don't believe we've seen a truly socialist society yet.

The second thing is that I believe that socialism will work if you consider it objectively. There are enough resources in the world to provide the basics for everybody. If we redistribute these resources, everybody can live with a roof over their head, have food in their stomach, get an education, have a job, and be provided for. Regardless of whether or not they can work, society as a whole will provide for them. There can be true equality and liberation for everyone. We must do it under a system different from capitalism, because capitalism has shown that it is not only unable to grant us equality and liberation but in fact thrives on our lack of them.

woman of power: What would you like to see happen with respect to white women and women of color forming deeper coalitions and working together more closely in the 1990s?

Kato: I would really like to see more coalition building. I think that it will happen; it is already happening. When we talk about forming coalitions, we want to form them around the issues of women of color. We want a coalition that is inclusive and democratic, so that all our voices can be heard and all our issues can be addressed.

Our issues as women of color are really everyone's issues. For example, when women build a reproductive rights coalition, I would like to see women of color and white women working side by side on an agenda that prioritizes issues of free abortion on demand, no forced sterilization, twenty-four-hour quality childcare, and rights for young women to decide what to do with their bodies. We need to rise from the bottom, as opposed to rising from the middle or the top, so that everybody can rise.

woman of power: In articles about your experience in Radical Women, you have said that one of the reasons that you found trust and friendship there was that you weren't asked to choose between your issues. Would you elaborate on that?

Kato: I began my activism in the Asian-American movement when I was in high school, and I always thought that there was something missing. I loved the work but I always thought that somehow my voice wasn't being heard. I didn't even know what feminism was, because there wasn't any, at that time, in the Asian-American community. Fortunately, now there is. I wasn't being taken seriously, partially because of my views, but also because of being a woman. I always felt somewhat incomplete working in the Asian-American community at that time.

And then when I found Radical Women and saw that women can integrate all these different issues, I began to realize that what was missing in my life was feminism. In Radical Women we raise all these different issues together, and I feel as if I'm in a place where I'm making myself whole, in the organization and in society generally.

woman of power: In connection with the idea of making yourself whole, how do you think your work releases a celebration of spirit?

Kato: One thing that really keeps me going is that when you fight with other people against any sort of injustice, whether it is something very minor or something very major, you see the best in people. In struggle, we push each other, we come together as a group to work for something that is better for all of us. It is that real sense of collective spirit and collaboration that gives me hope that people really do want to live this way. They really do want to live collaboratively instead of as individuals doing their own thing, because there is so much joy in working together.

I think activism brings out the courage in people. You push people; you get challenged; you win things together; you work for good things. I think that that is very, very rewarding. That is what really keeps me going, having the opportunity to see people grow and change and move forward.

woman of power: What is the source of your spirit or your energy?

Kato: I think it is my political beliefs. I'm Japanese American, raised as a Buddhist, and I was taught to try and make life better for everybody else. There is an element of sacrifice involved, yes, but we're here on this planet to do that. There are always things that need improving, not just for ourselves but for the community as a whole, however that community is defined. So I think I'm fortunate to come from that type of cultural and religious background and in having found a political group in which I'm really able to carry that out through political action and activism.

If you look around, everyone is trying to create a sense of community. White lesbians are trying to create a sense of community, a safe space. People of color do that and working people do that too. We have to create it for ourselves, because it is not going to be created for us. That is the important thing.

woman of power: What empowers you?

Kato: Working with other people empowers me. Frankly, it is being successful too. Success breeds success. I think it is very important to take a stand and to fight. In fact, that may be the most important thing, because of course you're not going to win all the time. You learn a lot from standing up and working together and it makes it easier the next time around.

woman of power: Can you talk about some of Radical Women's recent successes?

Kato: Yes, I can think of two examples. A couple of years ago, in San Francisco's Bay Area, we found out that the Nazi skinheads were planning an Aryan "Woodstock" on a ranch somewhere in the Napa region of California. We had only a week to organize people. When we arrived in the Napa area, we didn't know anybody there. We essentially went through the phone book and called up organizations or dropped in on them. In spite of negative publicity that there was going to be violence, a thousand people turned out to counter-protest the Nazi skinheads, only a few of whom showed up.

But I think the most rewarding thing was that a lot of people from the community came out in spite of all the press and the police and the local city government trying to raise their fears with messages to "Stay away, stay away." Those people in Napa decided that this was an issue important enough to take risks. And I feel that I had a part in helping to make that happen. I think that, in terms of success, you gain a lot of confidence when you see that you can approach people on the basis of shared concerns—Napa is in the wine country, and a lot of the people are middle-, upper-middle-class people—and you find that you can work together. That is a success story about working in coalitions that came together literally in a week.

Another success story is one that has lasted for nine years. Merle Woo, who is one of my comrades and a good friend, has been involved in an ongoing discrimination battle with the University of California at Berkeley. In two different instances she was fired from her teaching job for being an outspoken radical and an Asian-American lesbian. We formed a defense committee and generated a lot of publicity and support and we won.

And who are we but just a group of people who believe we are right and are willing to fight? We took on the University of California, the largest employer in the state of California, and we won. We're not supposed to be able to do that. We did it because we had public support. You can win.

I also think that our fight inspired other people to fight, too, people who wanted to fight but didn't quite know how. Because of the widespread publicity we generated, people would call us for advice about similar situations. So success builds upon itself. I think those are the things that keep me going. You feel like you're doing something, that you're making a difference. I think that is what it comes down to. Whatever we do, we can make a difference.

Our history as women of color has been to rebel and to fight back against any sort of tyranny. Our history has also been one of struggle and of victories. In spite of everything, in spite of the powers that be, in spite of the terrible things that have happened to us as groups of people, we haven't been defeated in the five hundred years since Christopher Columbus showed up. We're still here, we're still strong, and we're still moving ahead. So that gives me a lot of optimism. We have five hundred years of history that says that we haven't been defeated.

Earlier I was talking about historical crossroads. This is our chance to say that we want to make a different world. All sorts of social forces are in place to enable us to do that. Internationally, people are rebelling against the U.S. government or against U.S. imperialism.

Even in this country people are rebelling. And rebelling not just against the use of imperialism in other countries, but against any sort of repressive force. There are very positive actions going on that say to me that people are ready. They're ready to live a better life. And we're putting forth something that says, "Hey, check this out." And we hope you will check it out, because we know Radical Women is not going to make a worldwide revolution by ourselves. But we feel we have very powerful ideas. If we can get them out, people will take them and use them.

woman of power: Have you been in touch with women in any other international movements?

Kato: Yes. We have contacts in Canada, Mexico, and Europe. Radical Women is sending a delegation later this year to Eastern Europe to talk to feminists about what has been going on there, what they're fighting for, what they're thinking, what they're doing, and what they'd like to see happen. We also hope to give them some of our ideas about what has been happening here and to tell them what we've been successful with.

woman of power: How has Radical Women facilitated the leadership of women of color?

Kato: We women come to Radical Women because we believe that the leadership of women is necessary and that we need to make social change. To break it down a little more, we believe that women of color, because of our experiences, have a vision, an attitude about what needs to be done that allows us to work together. We all agree that we want to build women's leadership. But we're also a reflection of real life, so sometimes something racist may come up, but because we all believe that racism is detrimental, we can deal with it on that level. It becomes a little bit more objectified. It comes with more of a compassionate understanding that people may be acting more out of ignorance than because they are actually racist.

If you were actually racist you would never join Radical Women, because it wouldn't be tolerated. Why would you even want to be there? The same holds true for attitudes that are ablist, or homophobic, or otherwise oppressive.

Of course, everybody has different experiences. Some people have more experience about certain things than other people. We try to teach people. If a mistake is made, we deal with it. It doesn't always have to concern racism, and if it does, it doesn't always have to be a woman of color who addresses it. So we stick up for each other. I think that is what makes it easier to stick together and work together, even if we are very diverse, because we come together on the basis of shared ideas—that is why we joined the organization in the first place—so we're more eager and willing to change, too.

We try to live our lives today as we'd like to live them in the future. We're socialists, so we try to be socialists in our everyday interactions with people at work or with family or friends or other comrades or activists.

Attitudes take a long time to change, so we have to get started now.

———————•◆•———————

Excerpts from *Women of Color: Frontrunners for Freedom*

BY NANCY REIKO KATO

We Are The Ones We've Been Waiting For

The simple truth is that radical change—as in going to the root or source—ain't gonna happen without women of color at the very center of the struggle, teaching, administering, coordinating, inspiring, speaking, and drawing the movements together.

The truth is that women of color have a vanguard role to play in bringing together all the powerful movements for social justice and directing them towards a confrontation with the bankers and bosses. The reason is simple: no one needs change more than we do, for we bear the brunt of a vicious economic system that is sliding downhill fast.

Socialism: A World of Difference

There is a cure for capitalism—and it's called socialism.

Socialism is not the utopian, naive, unattainable goal that the bourgeoisie would have us think it is. It is a logical, scientific, practical and necessary alternative to capitalism. As the *Radical Women Manifesto* (also published by Radical Women Publications) states:

> *Socialism is a way of reorganizing production, redistributing wealth, and redefining state power in such a manner that the exploiters are expropriated and the workers gain hegemony so that a new era of cultural freedom and human emancipation may flourish on this earth. Feminism, like all struggles for liberation from a specific type of bondage, is a reason for socialism . . . and a benefit of socialism.*

Socialism reclaims the world's productive forces from the hands of individual capitalists and allows all of us to share equally in our planet's wealth. It is a democratically planned economy—we get to decide what will be produced and how it will be distributed. The society we can create under socialism can be anything and everything we want it to be because, hard as it is to imagine, it will be we—the long-silenced women, people of color, workers, and all the other outcasts—who will run the show.

Putting Our Ideas Into Action

Radical Women are the lucky ones, the woman warriors with an organization to back us up, with sisters willing to teach us, and whom we in turn teach.

In Radical Women, women of color and white women do stand side-by-side. It is an honor and a privilege to work with all my sisters in the organization—women from many races, of differing ages, mothers and grandmothers, lesbians and straight women, students, secretaries, bus drivers, electrical workers, computer operators, lawyers and doctors—who all fight racism, sexism, homophobia, and wage exploitation with the same ferocity, intensity and commitment as I do. Despite our diverse backgrounds, experiences, and cultures, we are *comrades*.

Leadership: The Essential Ingredient

One factor holds back radical change: the absence of leadership with the program, vision, determination, and grasp of history to bring together a disunited working class to challenge the pinnacles of capitalist power. This kind of leadership is the most precious possession of the dispossessed—a movement can never ever have too much!—and it is more sorely needed now than at any time in human history.

Leadership like this is never born. It is made—out of our individual history, experience, needs, and study. Radical Women is confident that from the ranks of women of all colors will emerge the leaders to carry the day for humanity. It's a tall order, but not impossible.

Think of it: women of color have survived almost five hundred years under the heel of capitalism in the Americas. And it has been our search for dignity, against the greatest odds, that has forged in us the anger, determination, and political consciousness that compel us to step forward to challenge this bankrupt and dying system. Together with all the others demanding a decent world, we will change the course of human history!

Notes

1. Kato, Nancy R., *Women of Color: Frontrunners for Freedom* (Seattle: Radical Women Publications, 1990), p. 6.

3

Homegrown Juju Dolls

RIUA AKINSHEGUN

Riua Akinshegun is an artist who is exploring how to turn pain into a creative and motivational force. In 1971, as a member of the organization The Republic of New Africa, she was shot in the spine by another member of the group and was not expected to live. Says Riua, "I became a paraplegic and was in constant pain for seventeen years. I was not a functioning person. But art saved my life. It brought me peace when I was in severe pain." Riua's sculpture, ceramic masks, traditional batik, and African wrap dolls[1] began to gain recognition as she continued to create art to channel her pain.

In 1989, an operation on her spine released Riua from her pain, and a whole world opened up to her. In June 1990, she traveled to Mali, where she staged a show at the National Museum; to Lagos, where she had an exhibit at the Ayota Museum; and to Senegal. "Homegrown Juju[2] Dolls— A Series on Chronic Pain and Healing" was her most recent show. She recently finished her autobiography, *The Seed of My Soul*, a work coathored with novelist Odie Hawkins.

It is Riua's hope to teach people how to manage both spiritual and physical pain, in order to reach their full potential whatever their present circumstances. To do this, Riua draws upon her near-death experience as a result of the shooting, her subsequent suffering, and the resulting near-homelessness and continual poverty she experienced while trying to survive on Social Security payments. "Everybody has some sort of pain," she explains, "whether it is physical, mental, or spiritual. I teach people how to channel their pain through art as a creative force."

———————•◆•———————

Going to Africa
Going to feel my ancestors
Going to walk the soil
Going to see the ocean
  the slave ships crossed
Going to touch the seed of my soul

Going to know the love of my hate
Going to know what made me a new race
Going home to see my mother. . . .
                    —*Riua Akinshegun, 1975*

woman of power: How do you think your work relates to the theme of this issue, "Women of Color: A Celebration of Spirit"?

Riua Akinshegun: I think I've always been spiritually concerned. I think it comes from my Indian and African ancestors. I've always been aware of my spirituality but I kept it in the background and became very focused on my political life. I think my interest in Africa was a natural progression for me after the sixties. I still feel that until Africa is taken seriously, African Americans are not going to be taken seriously.

When I went to Africa in 1975 and lived amongst the Yoruba, I really got into the empowerment of nature for the first time. It was the first time I'd ever known a religion in which the religious ritual wasn't centered in a building. It wasn't a one-day-a-week type thing; it was simply how you lived. It was every day within you: your eating, your sleeping, your dreaming. It was a whole different concept. Now I see my spirituality and my work as one. I wasn't an artist until after I was injured. I was thirty when I became an artist in Africa. I was always artistic, but I didn't think of art as a profession, for me anyway. Somehow I think, creating my art for me was like being the tool; I'm not the creator of my art. My whole thing is: art is a healing force. You've got to give that acknowledgment back to what carried you through.

woman of power: *You have used the word "channel" in connection with your work. Do you feel that your work is channeled?*

Akinshegun: Yes. You see, I was in serious pain for seventeen years and there were three things I could do to get out of pain. One was astral projection, or going internal. The second thing I could do to get out of pain was my art. The third was making love. Astral projection for me takes two forms—in and out of the body. The first time I experienced going out of my body was on the operating table after the shooting. When I experienced that first astral projection, I could look down at my body on the operating table and I saw the intravenous tubes and all the other tubes that were keeping me alive. I floated out into the hallway and went down the hallway and everyone was in the waiting room crying—my students and my family and everyone. And I was getting ready to go out the door but I kept thinking about everyone in the waiting room so I went back to comfort them.

My art could also get me some relief from my pain. When I go into my work, things just start happening. I incorporated the wrapping technique that was carried over from slavery here into my dolls because I wanted to put a little bit of history into the pieces. I'm just beginning to understand my last series of work. It's just coming to me now what I did, whom I created. I created three dolls in my last series, "Homegrown Juju Dolls: A Series on Chronic Pain and Healing," and it's been just recently that I've understood that one of my dolls, "Wisdom Past and Future," did all of my woeing, all of my nonverbal crying and mourning, for me. "The High Priestess" was for protection, and "Earth Mother" kept me grounded and in tune with nature.

I have arguments with the dolls as I'm creating. They want me to do something and I don't want to do it; I'm stubborn and I don't want to listen. And then finally I'll say, "Okay, I'll try it." And when I try it, it just fits. I don't even understand what I'm creating. It's been a year since I created them, and I'm just beginning to understand them. That's why I have a hard time releasing them and selling them, because I don't even know them yet. When they're ready to be released, they'll let me release them. It's very difficult right now because they're still talking to me, still telling me things.

I have also made some sculptures. I think I'm getting ready to merge my dolls and sculptures together, and do some larger pieces. I'm not quite sure what the medium will be, whether ceramic or even wood, it could be anything. Because I work in mixed media, I'm not restricted to anything.

woman of power: Did you begin to work out of the African tradition after you visited Africa? Do you feel that you've reclaimed or somehow reshaped those spiritual traditions into your own personal tradition?

Akinshegun: Oh, yes. When I went there, I was not trying to deal with the religions of the African people. I was just going for art and culture, thinking somehow that was separate. But one of the goddesses, Oshun,[3] the goddess of fertility, the goddess who protects women and children, just claimed me. I have never been claimed like that before. I became a daughter of Oshun. I would go to her shrine and talk to her a lot. I was very affected by how the people incorporate all the gods into everything. I met Ogun,[4] Shango,[5] all of them.

After a while, I understood that the African people were trying to be in tune with everything around them. And I find that if I can be balanced with nature, then things will work around me pretty well. Knowledge opens up for me. I try to listen to the Earth. I try to listen to the wind. I try to acknowledge everything respectfully, because everything has power. Rocks, seeds, everything.

When I was there, I had no idea about going into my body. My pain got so bad when I was in Africa that I had to withdraw, what I call "ignoring pain." So what I learned to do there was to go inside my body. I just started listening to my pain so that it would release me. I tried to make a friend out of it. Whatever I was doing, I would go inside.

These days, since the operation, my world seems so chaotic because when I was in pain I was so much in my body, so much in the physical world, that I tuned everything else out. The rest of my life was done through a veil, through a haze. The pain taught me to live in the immediate world, and I still do that because once the door is open it doesn't have to be closed. Now that I no longer have to spend so much energy on the pain, my concentration seems effortless, especially for my artwork. I can work for hours on end. While I was inside my body, sometimes for two or three hours, I couldn't respond to anything around me. People would be in my room; they'd be talking; I could hear them; I could follow the conversation; I could see; but if I acknowledged any of it or responded, the pain would just attack me. So I would just withdraw, and when I was withdrawn I got to understand my organs. I would review my day, and I learned to take time to do that every night. What that allows me to do is immediately take out nonsense, things that keep me unbalanced, or things that I said that were not quite correct. This daily withdrawal keeps me really balanced. And that's where I get my power and my spirituality.

woman of power: Do you think of it almost as a trance, what you had to do to ignore the pain?

Akinshegun: I think it's more like astral projection, but instead of going out of the body it's going into the body. During this last trip to Africa in 1990, I went to the Slave House in Senegal, the place where they held our ancestors before they were deported. It is in a place called Gorée Island outside Dakar. I lived on the Slave Island and the history just wouldn't leave me. For the first time in my life, I looked back through all those years of pain, and how I lived, and realized that even in pain I still lived a pretty healthy life. So I took my heart out and held it in my hand and just hugged it, for hugging people, for treating people well, for treating me well, for letting me look back at my life and recognize that my heart is a good place. I've never done that before, just held my heart. It wasn't just imagined, it was an actuality. It felt like something I actually did. I was sitting on my bed on the Slave Island and I was afraid but happy to be that close to my ancestors. I just sat there and rocked and smiled and I looked back at my life. Now I try to acknowledge all my organs.

We don't take enough time to acknowledge our bodies. I learned this through astral projection. When I was injured, I left my body many times during the three critical months following the shooting, and I have left it many times since. It has opened up many new concepts for me. I think we're all capable of learning them, but I think my being shot and thrown into this other world so rapidly accelerated the knowledge. I think we all have the potential to acquire that knowledge. We don't have to suffer or be near death to open those doors. I just think they open up quicker.

woman of power: How do you think your work helps to empower women in particular?

Akinshegun: I wanted to do something to put an end to seventeen years of chronic pain. And when I got ready to go into the studio to work, I kept thinking about chronic pain, chronic pain, and nothing would come.

So I looked at my life. And I saw that I tried not to live my life as a sufferer. I thought about what carried me through these seventeen years, and that was the healing aspect of it. So I changed the title of my show from "Chronic Pain" to "Chronic Pain and Healing." Most of my pieces focus on how to channel your energy. For example, my sculptures are sitting on pouches and inside the pouches are healing objects. These are woman guardian pieces called "The Guardian Woman I and II," "Malakia," even "Oshun." Those are some of the images of spirituality I pulled on to carry me through. So I did workshops with the Guardian Woman series for women. We all came together and talked about things in our lives that we wanted to focus on changing, and things that would motivate us in other ways.

For example, one woman lost her child in a fire. She was forty before she even had her first child, and she lost her. So we talked about how happy the child was, and that helped us to see that the important thing was to make the mother happy, because the child was fine. We said, "We've got to work on us." So she created a piece of sculpture that was so whimsical that every time she saw it she had to smile. And inside the pouch she put different things that had belonged to her daughter, so that she'd remember that her daughter wants to see her smiling.

I just did a similar piece on exercise. Since the surgery, I don't have as much movement, but it's okay because I have less pain. On one side, from the waist down, there is no feeling because they cut the sensory nerve and left the motor nerve intact in order to relieve the pain. So there's no muscle tone and I pull to one side, but soon I'll be going to physical therapy to work on that. Last year the pain was bothering me so much that suicide was becoming an option—I couldn't draw, teach, or read—all I did was rock constantly. Then I heard about this new technique with a seventy percent success rate, which has really changed my life. So I did this piece, and every time I see it, it focuses me on what I need to do.

woman of power: What do you envision for women of color in the 1990s?

Akinshegun: I hope that we get closer to nature, and I think we are already. We're strong, nurturing people. There's a serious war going on between men and women, and I hope that that begins to dissolve. In Africa, I told them, "Until African women are treated with more respect, Africa is going to be in trouble. African people will be in trouble." And I see that they are changing. It is coming to be. We must get a majority of the world's peoples to understand that women are the source of their power, to see that the concept that woman was made from man is totally illogical. We have to put the whole cycle back together.

Women of color must become friends. We have the same battles—we must become comrades. We must share our knowledge with our European sisters.

woman of power: Do you think that your art crosses barriers, contributes to the sharing of cultures and the building of communities?

Akinshegun: Yes. I think that art can be a force for coalition-building between women. If art is going to continue to be the forerunner of culture, then it must be connected to changing the world. In Mali, the artists were so excited to meet me because they said there were no women artists. At one show, some of the top artists said to me, "We're so glad you're here. Maybe the women will do art now." It is amazing how I would go around and ask, "Where are the women artists? I want to meet the women artists." First they'd tell me, "There are no women artists." "Are there any women sculptors?" "No." And I'd say, "Think hard," and they'd find me one. And then I'd talk to her.

I go there so they can see my work for several reasons. In many African countries, artists tend to repeat traditional art, so they're not dealing with new concepts. And so I hear people say, "It's great you are here because maybe they'll take this art out and do more," because my work is sort of unusual. I do the traditional work, but I also do other things. Every now and then, I can just stretch out and be free to do something totally unconnected.

woman of power: And that was an unusual concept to them?

Akinshegun: In Mali it was. In Nigeria that's not so unusual; they're pretty wild and pretty frantic, and I did get to meet the women there. The women be running the stuff! It's a little different there. It really varies among the cultures, so I think it's important that my work goes to Africa.

Most of all I'm trying to encourage African women to travel and to exchange, and hopefully there will be a couple of women artists coming to the United States and living among the artists here. I want to set up a program where I can take three women artists from here to Africa, live for three months and work. It's such an education. We will do that until the women artists meet us there, and then bring them here to work with us. That's where the growth starts. And we'll start branching out.

When I was in Mali I asked whether they had any female goddesses. They laughed at me. "There's only one god, Allah," they said. I traveled with another woman who asked questions about goddesses. They just laughed at her, so I said, "No, no, they don't understand what you're asking. You have to take it back further than Islam." So I asked, "What about the traditional African religion before it?" "Oh yes, there were plenty of women goddesses."

In Nigeria, they still identify with the goddesses, with Oya[6] and others. And they're in a much more frenetic place. The movement from Mali is much calmer, more peaceful and subdued; whereas in Nigeria, it's hectic, chaotic, and vibrant. And with that comes more changes. And the market women are so strong. You go there thinking that the women are seriously oppressed, but as you get into the culture, the women really run it.

woman of power: You were in the countryside as well as the cities?

Akinshegun: Yes, I was in small towns. That's where you get closest to nature. I lived in Ife—that's a small town in Nigeria that is considered to be the cradle of civilization. That's where I learned the real tradition. I didn't realize how traditional a style I was learning until I got to Lagos, the city, and they said, "She's an Ife girl," because when I did speak a little Yoruba, I spoke in the real traditional way. In Ife, I lived among the top artists, who are like priestesses and priests because they follow the old Yoruba ways where art and spirituality aren't separate. We talked about the *orishas.*[7] To me those artists were the forerunners of the culture, and they were very open. It was there that I had the most political conversations, where I could talk. In other places, I couldn't talk about my ideal society, empowerment, women's spirituality, and all of that. The elders, for example in Mali or Senegal, would consider it sexual for women and men to talk together like that—they don't even allow women to shake hands with men or to pray. Muslim women have to pray behind closed doors. They cook all day and then they eat alone or with the children. The separation of the sexes is complete. What I did was talk among the youth where the changes are gonna come.

Africans don't know who African Americans are. African Americans don't know where we come from, and the Africans on the continent don't know where we went to. It is as if that bridge was deliberately broken, and it is real strong and it needs to be reconnected. That's why I go there and try to educate. I tell them that we're Africans, and they say, "Yes, we heard about our people being taken away." Period. It ends there. So there's a lot of work to be done.

woman of power: How do you think women can celebrate our spiritual selves?

Akinshegun: By acknowledging it. By understanding it. By getting into it. Most women don't even know the power we have. If women would just look back at history and see how we've evolved, we could know that. But unfortunately, many women don't know that.

I think women need to unite among ourselves. Somehow the African woman is not being pulled into the feminist movement. I think that when we talk about feminism, if we can include the whole picture, that will help us to draw in African women. One of the problems is that during the sixties, when the Black movement became separate from the white movement, when the feminists became separate, and the disabled became separate, even though many of the techniques were borrowed from the Black movement, somehow feminism didn't pull in Black women.

Even so, African people are not yet strong enough to separate out as women. I can't separate and leave my child alone. Or leave the whole race alone. We're dying as a race. I think that we can start being a total vision and yet understand the need to pull together for that reinforcement.

How do we celebrate ourselves? By following our intuitive nature instead of pushing it back. If we can learn to listen to our inner selves and not worry about society's interpretation of things, that will free us up. Spirituality can't be separated from breath, let alone art. I don't pray; however, I try to live my life as a prayer.

Notes

1. African wrap dolls are made in the style used in the United States during slavery times. Bits of cloth are wound around wood or wire.

2. Juju means magic.

3. Oshun is the Yoruba Goddess of love, healing, and female energy; Queen of the River.

4. Ogun is the Yoruba wild man of the woods; a blacksmith.

5. Shango is the Yoruba lightning and thunder god.

6. Oya is the Yoruba Goddess of wine, water, fire, and rainbows.

7. *Orishas* is the Yoruba term for deities who are personifications of the faces of nature.

4

Building Coalitions in the 1990s

FLO KENNEDY

Flo Kennedy is a lawyer and a longtime activist in both the civil rights and women's movements. Now over eighty years old, Flo was one of the first Black women to graduate from Columbia Law School, in 1951. In the 1960s, she was a delegate to the major Black Power conferences and later founded the Media Workshop, the Feminist Party, and the Coalition Against Racism and Sexism. She is the author of *Abortion Rap*, and her autobiography, *Color Me Flo*, was published in 1976. Flo is the national director of Voters, Artists, Antinuclear Activists and Consumers for Political Action and Communications Coalition. She also hosts the weekly cable television show "The Flo Kennedy Show" (originally called "Liberated Women") seen in New York City.

woman of power: You have led a very interesting life—what sorts of interests or projects are you pursuing these days?

43

Flo Kennedy: I'm doing a weekly cable TV show talking about anything I want to put on, mostly women and families. Also, until recently, I was doing a lot with the Clarence Thomas nomination for the Supreme Court. I see Thomas as someone who climbed the ladder and pulled it up behind him. I was very much opposed to him and I was being real nasty about that. I didn't make many friends about it. The establishment loves it when we're horizontally hostile.

My travel in 1991 has included the National Black Congressional Caucus, along with some college campus lectures. And I'm beginning to work on the 1992 Democratic Convention.

I think that we women ought to have more national connections. In other words, I think that New York women ought to be more in touch with Boston women. Media is very important for oppressed people because that is where people can be reached. I want to see more women in media because I feel that one of the reasons women can be so easily manipulated is that so many work in their houses, and they are not in touch with each other. They watch media but media are not very generous about giving women opportunities to talk politics. They'll let us do comedy and they'll let us do talk shows as long as they aren't on anything important involving women. That lack of communication is a part of our problem. If the man says so, women can talk about endometriosis and blocked tubes and things like that. But the women don't just get on and talk to each other, for each other, about politics. And I think that's real important. Radio and television should be more like the back fence used to be: people would talk about the kids, and disease, and female trouble, and everything. So I think that the politics of women will change as we get more into media.

I think that media are, in and of themselves, very political. Women of color are particularly excluded because we are rarely on television—in a political context. There are lots of dancers and lots of singers but there is very little politics. I think we should informalize a lot of the print media. Women writers should not write so theoretically; they should interview more women about various issues including their feelings about "inconsequential" things. We do a lot of important writing, but we should also do some "unimportant" writing and have people whom we regard as unimportant say what they think as if they were talking on the telephone.

I think that when you ask women about legislation, it ought to be on a much more informal basis. You're usually talking to women who have degrees and I think that that's bad. I think that we should forget that women have so many degrees and talk to them about whatever they think about, the way they would with their friends or their sisters or their mothers when they call them on the phone—way down low, not so high falutin'. Women are so proud of their degrees and their posturing and their corporate level positions that they forget that they're just people, and a lot of the things that they care about have nothing to do with that stuff.

The attitude of the white society is exclusive where women's politics are concerned. Women are always there, but they are usually there to reinforce the premises of the culture which is antifemale in many respects. So I'm working on that—it's *all* political, but it's fun.

I think we should also focus on women in international media. I'm trying to get tapes of my TV show on feminist subjects to the women of India and Pakistan. I think we should focus on developing communication between women nationally and internationally, especially in the Middle East and Africa.

And then there is the whole abortion issue: everybody predicts that *Roe v. Wade* will be reversed, that the Supreme Court's agenda is going to be to push women's rights and civil rights, especially affirmative action, back to where they were before Jimmy Carter. And I think that there's enough truth in that to get to work on it now.

I'd like to see women talking woman-to-woman about politics. The politics of your kids, and the politics of your buying habits, and the politics of consumer boycotting. Don't forget that it was the Montgomery bus boycott that really made a turn to civil rights. It wasn't so much the government that made the change in the way that people are treated on campuses and all. I think we ought to focus on the ideas of Black women and Hispanic women and Haitian women. We need to understand that there's another whole voting group out there and we need to get their votes on our side in the next presidential election.

We've also got to focus on the way Black officials are treated. I think that New York Mayor Dinkins is being given a bum rap and my old friend from Kansas City, Barbara J. Sabol, head of the Human Resources Administration in New York, is treated so badly it's unbelievable. The trouble with these human services agencies is that they are full of people who are supposed to keep the blood off the floor so that the people at the top won't slip in it. And if you try to change the system they don't like it. There are always the people who get kicked in the ass and the people who do the kicking, and then there are the ones who apply the salve. People who are oppressed are often given their very own group to oppress. These human services people are supposed to wipe up the blood instead of applying a tourniquet.

We should focus on some of the Black women who have reached these heights. As Shirley Chisholm pointed out when she first went to congress, you get the sexism of your own group as well as that of the white establishment. We need to consider why Black women at the top get an extra dose of hostility. We need to focus on women of power, for example, Black female mayors around the country, and focus on their experience politically. Don't you think that might be fun?

woman of power: Where would you like to see women of color direct their energies in the next decade?

Kennedy: We need to fix it so that a woman of color doesn't get any more hassle than a man of color, or even a white man. I think that we've got to carry politics into every job where there's a woman of color. We also need to compare women of color who are at the top here with women in other countries, all-color societies, where the markets are dominated by women of color. I think we ought to focus on the women in the international scene as a whole, just to get an idea of what happens to the women in a nonwhite society, how they're different. Women of color should look at international politics in a different way and not buy the media's analysis of places like the Middle East. And women should be among the first ones to criticize Bush.

I also think that women in the Black community should join with the feminists. I've been criticized for being so cozy with the feminists whom most Black people see as mainly white, but it's not really true. And I think that women should become more political about everything—race, sex, affirmative action, everything—because, especially when we're not working in offices or our jobs are not real important and not well paid, we can afford to be brave in our politics. We have to understand that the most important thing that white women have to offer us is a philosophy of hostility towards people whose interests are not our interests and who don't have our interests on their agenda.

woman of power: How do you think deeper coalitions between women of color and white women can be formed?

Kennedy: Well, they will form automatically because Black women are going to college in larger numbers than ever before in American history. They meet and they are friends and they get to know each other. And otherwise we just have to understand that the men who are hostile to us, the white men of the mainstream society, are hostile to any movement toward the top. Many Black people are very hostile toward Black top officials because their circumstances have not changed to the extent that they had hoped. When they voted for Black candidates, they asked for more than they would have from a white man. If you vote for a white man, you don't expect much and you don't get much, and you don't get indignant. But if you vote for a Black person and you don't move from the projects to the suburbs, you blame them. I think that's a bad thing to do. We must have a greater sense of family, I think, than we have. We need to think more about the Africans and other people of color throughout the world.

Many Black women don't trust white women, but I do. I think the more we get to know each other on any basis, the better off we'll be. Coalition comes out of knowing people.

woman of power: What trends or goals do you see ahead for feminism in the 1990s?

Kennedy: I think the struggle will continue, and all struggle pays off, no matter what kind. There will be more working women, and the more working women there are, the more women will get together. The workforce is dominated by white people, so we will work with more white women every day in the office. If you work with people every day in the office, even though you're on a lower echelon, the fact remains that you get to know them. So the coalition happens automatically. Because more Black women go to white schools, there is further occasion to get together.

All people need to do is get together to know each other and like each other. It's hard to hate somebody you work with and see every single day. I think it will happen automatically. There is a great deal of coalition in the workplace and the more Black people and people of color get into the workplace, the more coalitions there will be.

In my opinion, the insider who is against your interest is a traitor whereas the outsider is the enemy. And I regard the white community as inimical to my interests for the most part. But I do think that there will be changes because we're infiltrating politics at the higher levels, and we're infiltrating the higher echelons of corporate structure and business. So we have to know more white people, and the more we know white people the more we will fight together on the same issues. There will obviously be a steady progression of coalition, because we won't be in the slave cabin while they're in the big house.

I think that in the 1990s, we'll go higher but we'll get punched harder. In other words, we have plenty of high places for women—there are women of color who are mayors and heads of major agencies at the urban level and in the cabinet—but they get a double dose of dumping on.

woman of power: Are you encouraged by the gains you anticipate for women of color in the 1990s?

Kennedy: Of course. More women of color are getting educated, getting angry, getting friendly, and marrying each other. Definitely there will be improvement and changes in friendship, love affairs, legitimate marriages, the whole works.

Oh, I think there will always be changes, but it depends on us. I think that if we play our cards right we should have some really exciting things happen during the 1992 Democratic Convention. I think we ought to informalize stuff. People like you and me have to help make it happen. We should criticize people as people and not as political people separated from the rest of us.

I like to encourage other people, and I expect other people to be active. I go to the college campuses and I talk and encourage people. The 1990s have hardly started. But I like to ask women where they would like to be ten years from now, and I like to make them think about what they might be doing and how they would feel about that. Education for women has been a wonderful thing, but it has also made women stress the aspects of life that change when you have a lot of education.

I think that most magazines are involved with women who are educated, and I just think that there's so much more to life than what educated women talk about to each other. We're all thinking about the same sorts of things, but less formally educated women think and talk more about real issues. It's important that some of us try not to be so literary. I think that a lot of things get lost with a formal education.

I'd like to see women run for political office, too. Running for office makes you deal with more realistic things. If more women ran for office, politics would become more realistic about everything that women need, about the fact that although much of women's work is underpaid, most of it is not paid at all.

woman of power: Do you see any signs of women's issues being integrated into the workplace?

Kennedy: Well, I think that they are integrated but not enough. I think that the issues should be integrated on the level of what women are really doing, and I think that women should get remuneration for what they're really doing. One reason that women are paid less is that we do so much for nothing. We have babies for nothing, we nurse the relatives for nothing, and we do most of the stuff that we do in the home for nothing. That tends to devalue the work that some people get paid for by virtue of the fact that it is done for free in the home. The main point is that the work that you do in the home is not valued because no one really cares if you do it. People only notice housework when it isn't done properly.

woman of power: Do you think that's changing now that women are making gains in the workplace?

Kennedy: No, I think that it's getting even less important. Now that women are involved in the workplace, work in the home really doesn't get recognized.

woman of power: In what ways would you like to see women of color and working-class women providing leadership for the women's movement?

Kennedy: Well, I think running for office is one of the better ways because the women will bring their problems to you. And the problems will be the ones they really think about. It's very important that women run for office, very important. I think that it's one of the best ways to effect change and be changed by the experience. The politician herself becomes educated by being in politics. To the extent that their concerns are different, and to the extent that they're not different, the women who come to support these women will see to it that their issues are heard. But there's very few women in politics, running for elective office. Not nearly enough. It's easy and it's fun and it's important and you can make money. I think that organizations like the Women's Political Caucus and the National Organization for Women are trying to encourage women to get into politics, and there is an increase in the number of women, but I just think that there aren't enough women doing it.

I think we'll see all kinds of changes in the 1990s. But the main problem is this theory that George Bush is a shoe-in for president. That's absolutely absurd; the man is almost crazy. My position is that we've got to get rid of Bush and act as if it's doable.

woman of power: Do you have a candidate in mind?

Kennedy: Jesse Jackson is the obvious candidate. Maybe we don't want him to be the frontrunner and so we believe him when he says he's not going to run, but if we really wanted him, we wouldn't listen to him when he says he's not going to run. And let's not forget Barbara Mikulski, the U.S. senator from Maryland, or Nina Totenberg, the legal affairs correspondent for National Public Radio. Almost any woman is better than who's in now. Almost any woman you can think of is good. And I think women should devote themselves to getting David Duke, that former Grand Wizard of the Ku Klux Klan who's running for governor of Louisiana, out of politics. I think women should devote themselves to getting rid of some of these inferior men. Every woman should pick a rotten man she wants to help get rid of, and run herself. We should look for socialist women, just about any of them. I think socialism has more women who are acceptable than just about any place you can think of. I think we should go into socialist groups and encourage some of those women to run. International Workers of the World has several women. I'm not of the opinion that you have to have special women. I think you've just got to go to the right place and anybody there will be good. Any of the women in the Revolutionary Communist Party. Tell them we want them to run. Just look at how everybody goes crazy if you talk about certain issues like Communism or lesbianism or revolution.

On a larger scale, to make more connections, we should go to Cuba. Get some women out of the Mohawk group in Canada. Get some of the South American Indian women. Look among Indians in Chile or Ecuador. Don't just look in the usual places.

I think we ought to have meetings every month, women of color meetings, lesbian meetings, all kinds of meetings. When you go against a society to do what you want to do, you develop a certain strength. And meetings help that.

We should encourage women who set goals for themselves, goals that are unpopular. We should encourage Deborah Glick, an "out" lesbian who recently ran successfully for New York state assembly.

If you study the consumer market, you see that the main power that women have is purchasing power. Every time someone makes you mad, you can go on a boycott. Women have three kinds of power—body power, dollar power, and vote power. We should use them whenever we can. Women need to use our money to support our politics. If you don't like the *New York Post,* don't just talk about how bad it is, boycott it. I think the boycott is a good way to express women's power.

woman of power: What do you envision for women of color in the 1990s?

Kennedy: I think that we need to look around for women of color who would make good leaders. Look to where people are helping to create a nuisance. And if it turns out to be women, get their names. And women need to write more, to let us know who's worth thinking about. Just write more about whatever people are thinking about. When you hear about a revolt by women of color or Native Americans, get their names. Find out about them; read their literature. Every time I think of a great idea, someone says, "Oh, you can't do that, that's Communist." Well, that makes me think that Communists must have a lot of good ideas. We ought to look at what they're saying in places like the Mohawk revolution in Canada. I think we should become intensely interested in Native American struggles. We're still thinking about old stuff, and we've got to break away from the usual stuff that you see and start looking at what society disapproves of. We need to listen to people who are rebelling and learn from them and join them. Every time we hear about a struggle we haven't heard about before, we should get to know all about it.

I think women should also be thinking about money and how to get money. We don't think enough about money. Women should stop saying what people want to hear, about nonviolence and the highest good, and all that kind of stuff. If we really believe in nonviolence we should be rebelling against the tax mechanism in this country, because these taxes support Pentagon violence.

woman of power: What do you think about the state of feminism in this country?

Kennedy: I don't think the feminist movement is alive and well. I think it's in a coma but we can revive it. It's like an uncooked biscuit, unfit to eat. It's like a piece of dough lying on a counter, but if someone decides to pop it in the oven, you might just see something happen.

5

Supporting Our Frontline Struggles

WINONA LADUKE

Winona LaDuke is Anishinabe, from White Earth Reservation in Minnesota. President of the Indigenous Women's Network and campaign director of the White Earth Land Recovery Project, she is involved in land rights and environmental organizing in the Native community. LaDuke also visits local classrooms to teach children about subjects such as geese migration, making maple syrup, and harvesting corn, culturally based units for early-childhood immersion programs.

The White Earth Land Recovery Project, a grassroots organization, has had several recent successes. They negotiated with a local electric utility company to put up a wind monitor the group had purchased in order to assess the feasibility of using wind as an alternative form of energy. The Project also joined a class-action suit against the Minnesota Environmental Quality Board, which had allowed the Potlatch mill near Cook, Minnesota, to expand, doubling its consumption of mill wood (an issue of great concern to forest people such as the Anishinabe) without filing an environmental impact statement; and they established a cottage industry called Native Harvest to diversify their income base.

———————•◆•———————

woman of power: Please tell us about Indigenous Woman *magazine.*

Winona LaDuke: Indigenous Woman is written by and about indigenous women. It is produced by an editorial collective, and we invite articles by Native women on issues of interest to our communities. Our intent is to present issues from the perspective of indigenous women because we feel that our point of view is missing in overall dialogue in the Native community and in the women's community. Our magazine is a forum for the Indigenous Women's Network, an organization comprised of individual indigenous women and organizations working on issues that affect Native women such as sovereignty, treaty rights, water rights, environmental issues, domestic violence, our rights in communities as indigenous women, health issues, and a whole spectrum of legal issues. The intent of our organization is to work toward empowering women to participate in political, social, and cultural processes, and to engage in bettering the conditions in our communities and the conditions of indigenous women. So *Indigenous Woman* is interested in profiling the struggles of our communities, especially from the perspective of indigenous women, and in initiating dialogue on issues of importance to our community as a whole.

In our premiere issue (Spring 1991), we featured an article about the Gwi'chin who are in the Arctic National Wildlife Refuge, the intended site of extensive oil development in George Bush's national energy plan. We also ran a story about the Innu women who successfully contested the construction of a large NATO base in Labrador and an article on Norma Jean Croy, who is serving a life sentence in a California prison for her alleged involvement in a shootout; she didn't even have a gun and she walked out with two bullets in her back.

woman of power: What do you consider the central issues of this decade for Native American women and for women of color as a whole?

LaDuke: Environmental issues are absolutely critical issues for the 1990s. For example, we are concerned about the dams being constructed in northern Quebec, Ontario, and Manitoba. These dams will devastate about 15,000 people, half of whom are women, totally changing our way of life, devastating the political, social, and economic systems that people have been relying upon for their culture. Environmentally, these dams cause massive devastation. In the mid-1970s, an area half the size of Lake

Erie was put under water, which essentially changed a river system into a reservoir system. Whole species of fish were destroyed. Hunting areas disappeared. Trap lines were lost under water. Herds of caribou died. And in terms of people's lives, this kind of development forces people out of a land-based economy into a cash-dependent welfare economy. It changes the terms of their relationship to society from self-sufficient or self-reliant to that of a marginalized people, at the edges of the dominant economy. With this change come social problems such as the disintegration of the role of women. When these big projects go in, there are huge increases in domestic violence and suicide rates, as well as other social and economic problems. That's an example that is repeated across northern Canada, in Saskatchewan and all through the Arctic—a series of huge development projects that are affecting northern Native women. These kinds of projects are of great concern.

Another issue of great importance is that of toxic wastes on Indian land. There are one hundred proposals for toxic waste incinerators (or dumps or factories or facilities) on reservations throughout the United States. The whole process of "development" says to our communities that we don't have anything ourselves. It pushes something on us and says that what we know and what we've done all our lives is no good. That's the first thing. The second thing is that it introduces a lot of health problems.

Other issues that indigenous women are dealing with are the process of reempowerment, taking back power in our own cultures and own communities, and rebuilding our communities. Those are key issues and they are also indicative of other indigenous struggles.

We also learn from other women's movements, particularly the Cordillera in the Philippines; the aboriginal women's movement, the Maori women's movement in New Zealand; and the ANC and South African women's movement. We have common agendas and common issues in that we understand our relationship to colonialism—we need to be challenging colonialism, getting it off our backs. We can also share things with North American women, and there's an important dynamic that exists, but I think that our priority in our work right now is to change the conditions that are devastating our communities.

woman of power: *How do you think your work releases a celebration of spirit?*

LaDuke: Indigenous cultures are rooted in spirituality. Spirituality is a part of our whole community and our whole culture, not separate. And so the majority of women in our constituency find that spirituality is an empowering part of our whole social movement. We engage actively in spiritual practice. Our spiritual practice, our relationship to the Earth, is what gives us the strength to engage in resistance.

woman of power: How can women of color bring together powerful social justice movements?

LaDuke: I think that it is really critical to understand that people of color as a whole have been divested of a lot, disenfranchised economically and politically for the most part. Obviously power in this country is being distributed on the basis of race and class, and women of color don't fit into that. As a result, we don't have a vested interest in the system. And because we don't have a vested interest in the system, we are in a better position to be critical of the system. We are also in a better position than a lot of other women to talk about real systemic social change because, for the most part, we are looking at the system from the outside. So because of that I think that indigenous women and women of color are in a crucial position in terms of formulating a new or alternative vision of society, from a feminist perspective as well as an overall perspective.

woman of power: How do you think that that leadership will be different, for the women's movement and other progressive social justice movements?

LaDuke: First of all, from my perspective as a woman who organizes in the indigenous community, the reality is that most of the indigenous women that I'm familiar with do not associate as much with the women's movement as they do with the indigenous movement. And that is basically because our cultural history and our whole experience comes from being indigenous people. That's our association. That's our total frame of reference.

The reality is that in our own cultures, in our own communities, when our social structures are intact, we are in a much better position than are women in the patriarchal, industrial society. The fact is that in traditional northern communities, hunting and trapping and harvesting communities, women play an equal role in the society. It's not a matriarchal as opposed to a patriarchal society; it's an egalitarian system where women and men are viewed as equals. When colonialism strikes into indigenous nations, women are marginalized from our own economies, from our own political institutions, and from our own social systems. Since we are never allowed to enter into the power structures of colonial, industrialized societies, we become marginalized, and we become essentially second-class citizens. We are given the lowest-paid jobs. We have no political power. We are divested of most of the forms of traditional wealth and social standing that we have in our own societies. Instead of trying to fight for an equal piece of this other society, most of the indigenous women that I work with would much prefer to regain, reclaim, and rebuild their own indigenous societies. And because of that, indigenous women that I work with are not, for the most part, organizing around "women's" issues. What we are organizing around are indigenous issues, one component of which is women's issues.

woman of power: When you do address women's issues within your community, what are some of the most important issues?

LaDuke: One example is domestic violence in the Native community. The statistics in Ontario, for example, indicate that eight out of ten Native women have been abused at some point in their lives. And the statistics in the state of Minnesota indicate that eleven percent of women in battered women's shelters in 1988 were Indian women. And Indian women are only one percent of the population. Historically, however, abuse and domestic violence are not a Native problem. The root cause of the problem is colonialism. Abuse comes from industrial, patriarchal society, because of the whole distribution of power in society in which Native men are abused and consequently abuse Native women and Native families. Native men are victims of the society that is oppressing them.

In addition to the social, economic, and political realities inside our communities, external factors affect us as well. For example, 83,000 Indian men were inducted or served during the Vietnam conflict. And in the Persian Gulf war, five hundred or so Lakota men served. Indians have the highest per capita enlistment of any group in the country. We've become totally militarized by the United States. Some communities feel that military service is implied in their treaty obligations, and there is also the reality that poor people and people of color are targeted by the armed forces recruiters. As we know, the majority of enlistees in the armed forces are people of color, and when those people return from Vietnam, or from the Gulf, they're suffering from things like post-traumatic stress disorder. They are returning to reservation housing projects, which are essentially ghettos on reservation communities, and when we know that, there is no mystery as to why we have domestic violence. We know that we have domestic violence because of a colonial situation.

woman of power: What do you envision for feminism in the 1990s?

LaDuke: I'm interested in the women's movement expanding the vision and the understanding of reality. There's a lot of really great thinking in the women's movement, particularly around the whole idea of the oppression by patriarchy. The next key step that needs to be taken is to understand the oppression from industrialism and, within that, understanding the power of women to undertake meaningful social change, and to look critically and supportively at what I consider to be front-line struggles, such as the struggles of indigenous people against industrialism.

I'd like to see the feminist movement and women in general make the connection between all the issues—going out there and really supporting the struggles against racism, the struggles of indigenous people, supporting our struggles as a way of dismantling the patriarchal industrial system.

woman of power: How do you think deeper coalitions between women of color and white women can be formed?

LaDuke: A clear example is in northern Wisconsin. Every spring, indigenous people—the Chippewas, or Anishinabe as we call ourselves—go out to harvest or spear fish. And historically, non-Indian people who are living in communities that are rife with racism come out and oppose Indian fishing on those lakes even though Indian people are entitled to fish according to treaty law.[1] For the past three or four years people have come out and thrown beer bottles at Indians, screaming at them and holding signs that say things like, "Save two walleyes—spear a pregnant squaw,"[2] really racist things that are targeted at Indian people, and Indian women in particular. This is the Selma, Alabama, of the north.

Broad-based constituencies, including church and social-justice groups and groups such as the Treaty Rights Support Network, have come forth to serve as nonviolent witnesses. This witnessing usually takes place early in the morning, around 5 a.m. when the spear fishers begin to fish. It is usually dark out and a group of Indians begins drumming and conducting ceremonies at the boat landing. The witnesses stand between the non-Indians (who have come to protest the fishing) and the Indians to prevent violence. Hundreds of non-Native women have already served as witnesses. When women talk about uniting to form coalitions against racism and oppression, this is the kind of thing that they can do. I think that they should be out there witnessing at places like the boat landings in Wisconsin. If you want to talk about racism in middle America in the north, that's where it is. I think that women should be there.

Notes

1. The Chippewa treaty in Wisconsin was signed in 1854.
2. Walleyes are walleye pike, a freshwater sport fish.

6

Children of All Nations

DHYANI YWAHOO

———•◆•———

Ven. Ugvwiyuhi Dhyani Ywahoo is a clan chieftainess of the Etowah Cherokee nation and founder and spiritual director of the Sunray Meditation Society. Trained by her grandparents, she is the twenty-seventh generation to carry the ancestral wisdom of the Ywahoo lineage. Her spiritual tradition is of the Etowah Cherokee people, holding the awareness of one truth behind the appearances of all of the religions that support nonviolence. A musician and a grandmother, she is committed to fresh air, pure water, and a world of peace for future generations.

Sunray Meditation Society is an international spiritual society dedicated to planetary peace that offers ongoing programs of education, service, and spiritual training. Its purpose is to bring together people from all walks of life to share and apply on the individual, family, community, and international levels the ancient wisdom of peacemaking rooted in the Etowah Cherokee and Tibetan Buddhist traditions. Sunray also works with Native American and Tibetan Buddhist communities to support and preserve their cultural and spiritual heritage.

Sunray is an affiliate of the Etowah Cherokee nation and is recognized as a Tibetan Buddhist Dharma Center of the Nyingma and Drikung Kagyu schools. Sunray practices embody these three ancient and intact spiritual lineages, whose common thread is teaching practical means to realize compassion and "right relationship" on Earth and throughout the family of life.

The Peacekeeper Mission provides training in personal and planetary transformation; its purpose is to bring forth peace in the hearts of the people and peace on Earth. It is rooted in the timeless Native American spiritual wisdom of "caretaker mind" and "right relationship" in the circle of life.

woman of power: As the spiritual director of the Sunray Meditation Society, much of your work involves peacekeeper training—how can we combine peacekeeping and social justice work?

Dhyani Ywahoo: The way in which we can most articulately be peacekeepers and still bring about change in unjust actions is to remember that every human being basically needs to be respected, understood, and cared for. The light or the potential for understanding exists in each person. So the first step in reconciling the appearance of differences or different understandings is to find the place where we have a common view. Once we see where our common view is, we see the ways in which we can energize that common vision. Then we notice the different ways in which we might wish to move with the problem.

For example, in terms of the abortion rights issue, everyone wants to preserve life, everyone wants to care for life, and mostly people think that they care for children although our culture basically mistreats children and women. On both sides of this issue—the so-called pro-life position and the so-called pro-choice position—the central issue is the quality of life for all those individuals. There is a common view that we all respect life, and then the point of divergence is where those who claim that abortion should be illegal do not really address the issue of poverty and the struggles of the mother who can't afford to feed her child, or the despair of the child who is not wanted and not able to receive the benefits that she or he needs such as clothing, food, and caring family. At that point we find that there's a different path.

It seems to me that the most important issue is not abortion but how we show our care and concern for those who are feeling bereft of hope or who are unable to become part of a system that will give them dignity, a place to live, and enough food to eat.

So being a peacekeeper is essentially seeing first where we are alike. Basically, every human being wants work, a good home, enough to eat, good company, and to be respected. All around the world we are the same. And I have a feeling that even animals are like that. I know that the dogs and the horses where I live, if they sense that they are not respected, or that one is valued more than another, their feelings are hurt. Because we all want basically the same things, we can look at ways in which we can bring this about. The first step, we understand, is caring for our family, our friends, our neighbors, and our coworkers. Rather than taking a pro or con position, we find ourselves thinking more of "and" rather than "but," thinking, "We can do this together, and we can try it this way," so that the various perceptions and the different views can work harmoniously.

How do we establish communities that are loving, where women can feel secure and safe and know that their efforts will be reciprocated in an equal manner, where males will do the same amount of work in building family relationships? We see the common view. How do we assist one another in supporting life rather than in being for or against? This is one area in which people perceive injustice, yet no one is speaking clearly of how to create the field of justice, which would be to give women and children priority in education, job training, and support systems, which have been deeply eroded over the last twelve years.

There are other kinds of injustices also. There's the injustice of women and men doing the same work for unequal pay. Women's worth is not as well received or recognized as men's, although women are the ones who give birth to everyone. It is assumed that a woman supporting a family needs less to live on than a man supporting a family—that's obviously an incorrect view.

How do we change it? The changing occurs at a very deep level, by being thankful for the gift of a human body and recognizing how difficult life is to obtain and how precious it is. Change also comes when we are willing to say that we will support what's truly respectful. There are now companies that have good employment practices in terms of the treatment of their personnel, female and male, and who provide childcare. All of us can express our appreciation and support for the mindfulness that is inclusive of the whole family by purchasing products made by these companies.

woman of power: Can you say something about how women of color are reclaiming, reshaping, and creating new ways of celebrating spiritual traditions?

Ywahoo: I look around and it's really quite amazing what black, red, and yellow women have been able to survive over so many generations. For thousands of years, women of color, the women who keep ethnic traditions and who grow the food, have provided a foundation for life with their care and their nurturing. We do our best to sustain our families in this industrial culture, in spite of laws that are still repressive to women and children. We continue to grow.

The voice of the woman is a voice of inclusion and invitation in that we choose to call forth the best from our children, for our children. If and when we choose to take responsibility to train the future generations, let us become more mindful and skillful in expressing patterns and means of resolving difficulties. The voice of inclusion is the voice that gives everyone an opportunity to win and every voice a chance to be heard. The best loved grandmother is the grandmother who listens to each of the children and recognizes each child's unique view and inspires the inherent gifts of those she meets to flower into right action. So the very fact that Native American culture still exists, the very fact that the indigenous cultures of Africa and the indigenous cultures of the East still exist, illustrates how the mother's storytelling, her knowledge of life and death, and her preparation of food are her most special gifts.

It is apparent to me from the numerous requests I receive from all around the world, that the world is asking in a very strong way for the teachings of women of color, of traditional women of ethnic cultures. Also, many governments are expressing the desire to have deeper understanding of means of reconciliation and I think everyone is deeply concerned for the future as they watch the ecological collapse of Eastern Europe and the Ural regions of Russia. So, as women of color, we have a special opportunity to reveal the mother within ourselves and within others through our actions, especially through our moon cycle and our relationship to the pulse of the Earth, to which women are a little more sensitive. As we talk more about this energy of cycles, and there's more scientific exploration to substantiate that our middle, right, and left brains do pulsate in rhythm with the basic ground of the Earth pulsation, more people can feel connected. When we look at all the cultures that still maintain the drumming practice, we see that this is a very powerful medicine for females and males to come again to right relationship with the cycles of the Earth pulsation. That's a most direct way in which people can see the special gifts of people of color.

When I think of women of color, I also include indigenous women such as the Ukrainian woman who still knows about herbs and midwifery; the Bavarian grandmother who still remembers how to leave offerings for the little people, the fairies; and the Scandinavian mother who remembers the meaning of reindeer moss as a medicine. We're talking about women of color because this issue is dedicated to women of color, but at the same time I recognize that the colorful wisdom of all women around the world has been inhibited, and through that process great suffering and despoiling of the Earth's beauty has occurred. It is now time for all women of the colorful mind, who are aware of the cycles of night and day and the dance of the moon in her tides, to arise.

The medicine of the women of Northern Europe is the memory of the herbs and the medicine of the trees. The medicine of the women of much of Africa is the medicine of the pulse that brings the heart back to its natural rhythm. The medicine of the women of the East is the medicine of sacred ideals. The medicine of the women of the Middle East is the medicine of sisterhood. And the medicine of the red women of the western hemisphere is the medicine of survival, adaptation, and bio-resonant interaction with the environment.

woman of power: Where would you like to see women of color direct their energies in this decade?

Ywahoo: The most important work that we have as women of color is educating our children to take pride in their ethnic origins, tracing the roots of our family history, and reclaiming all of the children who have become lost to drugs and whose parents are unable to show them how much they care. I would like to see places of sanctuary: small, self-sustaining communities where people of color can share their myths, special teachings, and medicine so that the young children who have become lost in the cities, and lost in drugs, can find a pathway to their own inner light.

I would like to see these places of sanctuary be self-sustaining communities where we might first help the young people to detoxify, to realize that they are indeed worthy of life, and to rebuild those pathways to happiness that may have been occluded or cut away by abusive or oppressive actions. Sometimes just going to school is abusive and oppressive.

These places of sanctuary would allow young people to realize that indeed they are important, that they are our future, and that their efforts make a difference. One of the ways that this can be accomplished is through the practice of ethnic crafts, where you can conceive of an idea, visualize it or draw it, and then actually build it. This can be done in beadwork (where designs sometimes come from dreams), or painting, or sculpting, or making pots and dishes that are functional for the community's use. In this way, a young person recognizes, "I can do something."

So I think that's a first step. And then a deeper step is to reclaim that divinity; to let them know that whatever errors have been made, any of us can return to the bosom of the Mother Earth when we recognize our errors and are willing to correct them. There's a big medicine in forgiveness. When we forgive, we are saying that we recognize that the ways in which we related in the past were inappropriate. Then, in this moment, I say to you that those past relationships are over and we establish a new field of relationship. We make our sacred dance ground, a sacred space that is really made of permeable membranes rather than walls, so that we can understand and communicate with one another at a rate that is consistent with our own inner rhythms. So many people are harmed just because those they love and work with do not understand that their rhythms are different.

In our tradition we say that there are basically seven types of people and they correspond to particular stones. These seven types are: quartz, which corresponds with the concept: "I will, I see"; ruby: "I understand, I build"; topaz: "this is how it's done"; jasper: "it is done in beauty"; emerald: "the wisdom of particulars"; rose quartz: "principles and ideals"; amethyst, stone of the peacemaker: "we change and grow." For example, there's the quartz kind of person; they move straight ahead; they say, "dit, dit, dit, dit." The quartz type of person has a very fast rhythm; they say "I see, I understand" and they do it. Like the quartz stone, they amplify the idea—as we know, quartz is the basis of our telecommunication, carrying ideas all around the world. The ruby person, on the other hand, is the person who considers all things in relationship, recognizes the ideal, and is the most concerned with the possibilities. If you're a ruby person, you see how everything is related and your voice is more like, "ah-woooooo, ah-woooooo," and your rhythm is more like a wave caressing the shore. That "dit, dit, dit, dit" person and that "ah-woooooo, ah-woooooo" person may have very few meeting places. And then there's the opportunity to recognize the places where you can meet and cultivate them.

I've just come back from a really wonderful visit with Native American women in the Taos area and we were talking about these same things. How can we help our children? How can we help the Earth? And we recognized immediately that the first thing is appreciation. We made prayers and offerings to the Earth and the sky, the Above Beings and the Earth Beings. The Above Beings we call *adawis;* they are angels. They are our most refined wisdom potential. We made offerings that this wisdom potential may take root in our lives. We made prayers and offerings to the Earth that the roots of wisdom may grow and that we may show our appreciation for the gift of life. We let ourselves reconnect with her pulse through spiritual practices and through purifying ourselves. And then we began to consider: How have the children become lost? How have things become so confused? And we saw that it's because they're taken from home; there are many hypnotic suggestions offered to them by the dominant culture and we must show the children how to recognize their own minds or they will become confused. So we did such practices, and we agreed to teach these practices to all the young people we meet—some of the women work with large numbers of young people. And we also cultivated the universal language of the heart, so that even when the words are not easily heard or trusted, because the child's trust has been stomped on, we can still reach one another's hearts through this pathway of reconciliation.

There is a lot that we, as women, can do, and it seems to me that the first thing that we have to do is reclaim our children. We can think of solutions like these places of sanctuary, and whole communities where first the children come, and then, when they are ready, their parents come to learn how to reparent themselves in order to parent their children. Too often children are hurt by parents who were hurt as children, and the greatest menace then is letting the children lead us. So the children show us that they're ready to be healed and then the parents recognize what steps they need to take in the healing process.

The Taos women and I have this dream that we call Children of All Nations, places close to the city where children can come and begin talking. And as they're ready to put aside their attachment to substances that are defaming the inner light, ready to leave the city and put aside blame of others, ready to take responsibility for bringing their own wisdom forward, they will be able to come to a place of sanctuary. After having regular visits and tutoring and counseling close to the city, they would go to a village where they would begin growing their own food, doing crafts work, and learning whatever it takes to fully communicate in this world. That means learning computer sciences, math, writing, and the philosophies of many cultures. The myths or the stories that are told by each of the indigenous groups will also be included because they provide a special path for healing. So this is our hope, that we can make a difference in this way.

woman of power: You have often talked about making connections between different traditions, such as the Tibetan, African American and Cherokee. How can we foster or affirm those connections?

Ywahoo: First we need to realize that every ethnic culture and every religion is based on the principles of nonharm and respect. They are all basically expressing one truth, and the truth takes many forms according to the culturalization of the people. We can also further foster good communication and respect for difference by seeing what are the common factors, what are the hopes, and by ongoing dialogue. However, because the rituals of each religion are distinct, they ought to remain as they are. There's no need to mix different rituals together because that can be dangerous. It's like mixing different herbs together—one does that with great care. It is better to understand the particular view that arises in each of the world's religions and to understand that whatever our family of origin, it enabled us to get this far. We can affirm those connections, understanding something about the religion we're born into, and then make clear choices about what is the appropriate spiritual practice to uncover that potential wisdom we all have.

woman of power: Do you have any advice for political activists about how best to follow a spiritual path and do political work?

Ywahoo: It seems to me that there's really no difference between spiritual path and political action. When we act out of compassion and consideration for the present and future generations, that is the wisdom of a compassionate caretaker. The most important thing I've learned over the years in terms of political action is that there really is no "them"; it is about "us." We're all part of the dance and I find that it has not really been effective in my life to point out the differences or the injustices with anger. I think that to talk from the place of what is appropriate and beneficial for everyone in the long run makes for a more clear path of communication.

People have a lot of energy and it's for us to give them a clear direction. One of my colleagues in San Diego works with Chicano gang leaders. She gave them some land and said, "Here, make a garden. You can grow food and you can feed whoever you want with it," and that gave the young people so much pride. They made their garden and they feed whomever they want and they are fighting less with each other. We can seek support from one another, so that those kids who once fought one another now weed a garden together, because basically people want to do something good. I would like to see a sense of volunteerism applied in our culture. It would be wonderful to volunteer with our neighbors to correct the problems in our neighborhoods. Even in the inner cities, people can volunteer and build gardens together.

The garden is also our own minds. We can also weed seeds of confusion from the garden of our minds, seeds of feeling victimized, and seeds of feeling that there's something to fight. There's something to change and something to improve. The moment we feel we have an enemy, then that enemy has power over us. The moment we begin to see our views converge, we can find a common pathway. That's making something more clear.

woman of power: *What is your source of spirit or energy? What empowers you personally?*

Ywahoo: Just about everything. My maternal and paternal grandparents are my heroes in that they overcame great odds and still maintained their inner integrity. That was a good model. I realize now that they wove the basket that is my life, and they helped me to weave a very sturdy basket.

Then, as I grew older, I realized that if my gift was to come through, I needed roots. I needed to have children myself. I understood that. The first child, a daughter, was born alone. I delivered her myself. I was in a labor room and the nurses changed shifts and forgot about me, and it was good because I couldn't have had her with them there. And that was very, very special. That tying of the cord, and her looking into my eyes, and us holding each other. That really confirmed for me the belief that there is reason to live and reason to make things better, for her and for those who would come after her.

Then when I had my second child there was another awareness, because she had a difficult birth and was deprived of oxygen for a very long time. I was told that she was retarded and blind, but I said, "I don't accept this." They said that I should institutionalize her because she was going to be severely brain damaged. I said, "I don't think so," and after a month I took her home and I would swing her around and rock her, turn her upside down and rock her, turn her this way and that way and rock her. Then, when she was about two years old, we realized that she could see. At about two-and-a-half, she began to walk; and at three she talked; and then at twenty-one she graduated from college with honors. So we can always make a difference. Of course, she made new pathways in her brain and the swinging her around helped her.

With the third daughter I realized: ah, how wonderful, how wonderful, here she is and I can see all her ancestors in her. So tiny and so strong and so perceptive. And then, eighteen years after her, I had a son. From the beginning he was looking and wanting to know and calling for explanation and wanting to act. And with my grandchildren, I see wondrous things too; each one has a remarkable view and unique way of being in the world, and I can see how all our relations flow in them, so that really makes me feel very good.

I also have the good fortune to do the kind of work I do, which is to tap the wisdom in everyone's heart, and to show others how to do it, too. I have the good fortune of meeting incredibly dynamic and bright people, many of whom have come through what appeared to be insurmountable obstacles and found their truth and are able to live it. So I'm fortunate that I continually meet good people, just as I met the women on the reserve in Taos and had a good time, a good feeling in that community, and in the larger community, too, with non-Native people. In this way, I see my family everywhere, and what was not perfect in my family of origin, I see ourselves, in the moment, perfecting. That's wonderful. Also, the multiracial diversity of my family members really gives me a sense of relationship with any kind of person, any race, any religion. I'm very thankful for that.

woman of power: How do you think white women and women of color can form deeper coalitions to work together more closely in the 1990s? How can trust and friendship be fostered?

Ywahoo: This is a really important question. I know that a lot of my Native sisters are very shy and uncomfortable about non-Native women. And a lot of my Black sisters are very shy and uncomfortable, and also my white sisters are shy and uncomfortable. The pathway of understanding is to first appreciate our diversity and to learn as much as we can without being intrusive about our different cultures. For example, in Native tradition, we have a special relationship with elders. We don't particularly ask questions, we sit and listen so that whatever is a question within us becomes revealed within us through the process of our being together.

I know that for some of my Euro-American sisters this can seem unbearably slow. And so we learn to respect our different rhythms and to gain a bit more trust. Trust is built over time. The most precious area of establishing trust is working together as equal partners without either one having the idea that they have something particularly special to impart to the other, an attitude that causes, I think, some unhappiness and can sometimes resemble preaching. Exploring our ethnic dance, whether it's a Polish polka, or dances to Yemaya,[1] or the dances of Tara,[2] or the Buffalo grass dance,[3] is a way in which we return energy to the Earth and awaken our minds a bit more to recognize just how deeply we are all related.

woman of power: What direction do you see the spirituality movement taking in the next ten years?

Ywahoo: I think people will go back to respecting nature, to being as self-sufficient as possible, and to simplifying their lives as much as possible. As I was saying earlier about Children of All Nations, I think that this idea of a village of sanctuary, or peace villages as they are called in our tradition, is very important. Cooperatively, people are finding land and forming co-ops with those who have other skills—food growing, water management, educating young ones, house building, crafts that can be traded with other groups—and such co-ops will provide great help to people who are returning to the land, because the cities can no longer sustain the vast numbers within them. And as we see the economy going through further changes, people are simplifying out of necessity. If we have some land with a few friends where we can grow food and live in a cooperative way with respect for each other's privacy, that's a good beginning.

woman of power: Are you encouraged by developments within the spirituality movement?

Ywahoo: Let's put it this way: I'm hopeful. I also recognize that those who have previously denied a relationship with the Earth as a living being are now beginning to wake up. They see that the weather patterns in the Ural regions of Russia are being altered in such a way that the very winds have changed and great areas have become desert. I sense in many people the large fear that arises when you see that your previous view was out of balance. I pray now that people will have the courage and the willingness to bring it back to balance.

Notes

1. Yemaya is the Yoruba goddess of water, birth, and awakening consciousness.
2. Tara is the Buddhist goddess of compassion.
3. White Buffalo Woman is an example of compassionate form who gave rituals such as the Buffalo grass dance to the people to renew their hearts and to renew the prairie grass.

7

Creating a New Cultural Etiquette

AMOJA THREE RIVERS

Amoja Three Rivers, an escaped New York cabbie living in the hills of Appalachia, is a craftwoman, a coatpuller, and an African Native American herstorian. As cofounder of the Accessible African Herstory Project, she works to fulfill the driving need to find out the truth about the ancestors and then tell it. She is the author of *Cultural Etiquette: A Guide for the Well-Intentioned,* a pamphlet designed "to help people avoid the pitfalls of unwitting racism and anti-Semitism. It seeks to help those with good and righteous intentions to refine their behavior and attitudes bred in cultural ignorance."

Amoja and her partner, Blanche, are involved in Market Wimmin, a business in the ancient tradition of West African market women. They are currently planning to establish a women's conference center to be run by and for women of color but open to all women. Shakti Root Conference Center would include an Institute for Ancient African Herstory and related subjects, a place for women to study African herstory and explore their own herstory. The center would also offer a library and video library and a place for women to make retreats, study, and heal.

———————•◆•———————

woman of power: You travel across the country as Market Wimmin, and you visit many women's festivals. What perspective can you offer on women in community?

Amoja Three Rivers: First of all, I would like to pin down a definition of the word "community." A community implies shared goals and values and a commitment to helping each other out. When I think of the word "community," I see a women's "culture" evolving, especially a lesbian culture. I have been doing a lot of multicultural work at the Womyn of Color Tent at many different women's festivals, including the Michigan Womyn's Music Festival, the East Coast Lesbian Festival, and the New England Women's Music Retreat. From the beginning, I sensed that something was happening at these festivals that I wanted to be a part of, something really magical. I began to see that a festival was more than just a "party." These festivals became microcosms of the world, places where we worked things out and experimented with cultural change and new ways of living with each other. And that was really exciting!

But what was missing was women of color and women of color's perspectives. At some of the very first festivals that I went to, I saw that other women of color were also having trouble with this. We were excited by the prospect of having a women's culture together, but we also needed to figure out where we fit within all of this and what we wanted for ourselves. And what we wanted for ourselves initially was pretty much what other women had at women-only events—a space together, alone, where we could relax and figure out what it was that we needed to be doing for ourselves. We needed more women of color there; we needed something within the community that made us feel like we were part of the community.

woman of power: What kinds of community-building work have you been particularly impressed with as you travel around the country?

Three Rivers: Traveling and networking are some of the things I like to do best. I like to gather flyers and names and information about whatever women are doing and to tell other women what is happening because it is exciting to see it, and it is exciting when you share it too. I see a lot of continuity and growth from year to year. The women's festivals seem to build on one another. The women at women's festivals have really done a lot of homework as far as trying to make things more multicultural and accessible, and they are becoming more aware of all the "isms" all the time. I am very impressed by the work that women have been doing. There are new women each year at the festivals but there are enough women from earlier years that there is continuity; they keep the work going so that the ideas can definitely grow. Women did things and said things a few years ago that they wouldn't dream of doing now at certain festivals.

I think the atmosphere of antiracism really makes women run something through their brains before it comes out of their mouths. They double-check thoughts, especially when they pertain to anybody's race or culture or any other area of difference. I've heard, too, that some women are afraid to say anything at all anymore. I don't think it is anyone's goal to make anybody else uptight, but on the other hand, it is not a bad thing to think before you speak. I myself find that I need to do that whenever I'm around people I'm not used to being around, because I'm afraid that I have absorbed things that I don't even know I have absorbed. I know that I have absorbed many bad ideas that I did not need to absorb, and I do like to run things past my brain before I speak. Many other women are doing this now, too.

I'm also encouraged by what I see as the willingness of women to get down into the mud together and roll up our sleeves and just fight it out. And even though it is painful and there is some crying and gnashing of teeth, there is a willingness to work things out, to work them out together and allow ourselves to feel vulnerable, to feel the possibility of pain and be committed to really working things out. I have come to realize that this is something important to have in the women's community.

woman of power: Do you find that these changes extend to other areas of the women's community?

Three Rivers: It seems that the microcosmic situations have seeded the other parts of the women's community and in that way I *have* found it. For example, the antiracism work that I have seen white women do at the festivals started largely because we were pushing them and complaining and carrying on. I see the work that they started within these festivals spreading out into the rest of the world. It's not only that these women go back to their communities and hold antiracism groups; many of them also work in agencies for social change and in universities and bookstores, and they are going back and seeding the culture at large.

Women of color do a lot of networking and establishing ties with one another all over the country and internationally as well. Just having the opportunity, in places like the Womyn of Color Tents, to see what other women of color are doing in their lives and at the festival means that when we go back out into the larger world we can take that feeling with us. For example, when I see a sister doing something that I don't think I can do, just knowing that she's a sister like me, then I know that if she can do it, I can do it, too! It's a very simple equation, but it creates a powerful new mindset.

woman of power: What allows people to feel that they can do this work together?

Three Rivers: I think, for instance, of the areas that have been set up for the needs of differently-abled women at the Michigan Womyn's Music Festival and the East Coast Lesbian Festival. Just having an area that you feel is yours is one of those changes that has made this kind of communication possible. So I see the commitment to change and grow demonstrated in actions rather than just in words.

As a woman of color, I feel a certain safety in the Womyn of Color Tent area. I feel safe enough to be angry. If I really had given up on a particular festival, then I wouldn't even bother to show my anger. I just wouldn't be around. But if I feel that the producers and the workers at a festival have a certain commitment to working for real change, then I feel safe enough to get angry and to share the anger. Then, when I see the women towards whom the anger was directed be willing to discuss it and go through the whole process, it all seems worth it. I'm encouraged by the fact that we are willing to do this work with each other because you cannot sweep a room without stirring up the dust. And this culture is terribly dirty!

woman of power: What makes it possible for you to do this kind of work? What empowers you?

Three Rivers: Growing up in America has made me feel powerless for most of my life. I had this feeling, although not even consciously, that nothing I could say or do or feel would matter, because, you know, it's the white boys' world out there. But being part of the women's community, of the lesbian community, in places like festivals and conferences and different communities around the country, makes me believe that my feelings do matter. I have seen that my ideas do matter because I have the space to implement them and have them supported. I also have the space to make mistakes; and I see other women making mistakes and getting up and trying over again.

The women's community is full of role models who are really empowering for me. I keep going back to my experiences with the Womyn of Color Tent, working with other women of color, women who are more like myself. Seeing things that they do, the support that they can give me and the support that we give each other, makes me feel that I can do anything that I want to do.

woman of power: What has it been like for you to claim your own cultural identity and then work with other women from diverse backgrounds?

Three Rivers: It has been really exciting. Some of it has been painful, but mostly it's exciting, especially when I have the opportunity to meet really strong spiritual women and be part of a setting that helps us to grow and to learn who we are.

As people of color, a lot of us are trying to reclaim cultures that have been interrupted. As lesbians, in particular, we are trying to figure out how we fit into our traditional cultures, what those traditional cultures are, and how all of this fits into the lives we are living within the women's culture. We are on a path of exploring, experimenting, and reclaiming, and we are getting power from that process because we're finding out who we are deep within ourselves. And we're finding out who we are in relation to each other, too.

I have seen African women drum for Native American women. I have seen African women and Asian women drum together and make a new sound and a new excitement. It's also very exciting and enriching and educational to understand the kinds of things we have in common and the kinds of things that are different among us. For example, there was an aboriginal woman from Australia at the Michigan Womyn's Music Festival last year. It was so wonderful to meet her and feel sisterly toward her, not only to recognize her, but to *feel* the things we had in common. She was a sister!

woman of power: Do you think it is because the festivals are somewhat intense or ritualized experiences that women are more receptive to changing themselves in those situations?

Three Rivers: Definitely. There's something magical that goes on at the festivals. I felt it from the first time I went to a women's festival. Part of it was the absence of male energy. I didn't even know that there was that tension in my life until it wasn't there anymore. And then that change allowed something else to happen. So the women-only space allows women's energy to grow, and then there's something else that happens, too.

I'm a herstorian and I feel a call from ancient women; I feel old voices and desires and meanings. And it isn't only me; other women sense these voices and feel the need to hear these old voices. I think that when women have a setting all our own, we let the voices come in clearer—the voices of the matriarchies that have been lost, of the women's lives that have been lost. I believe that the desire that those women had to make their culture known to us today in the present is something that they psychically sent out into the future. And being in a women's place puts us into a unique position to be able to hear them.

woman of power: In Cultural Etiquette, *you talk about how we are all manifestations of the Goddess's effort to know herself. How does your spirituality inform your work?*

Three Rivers: I wrote the *Cultural Etiquette* guide because I was tired of getting my feelings hurt by people whom I didn't think were intentionally evil. I was also tired of explaining things to people over and over again because it is painful to talk about these things. I also believed that this women-energy I felt was shared, particularly at intense events like the festivals, and I wasn't really willing to let that go just because some women were ignorant. So I thought, well, here's a chance to "pull their coats," which is an African American way of saying "get their attention."

I am an African Native American woman. I feel that we can each share a connection as well as an identification with other humans that hovers beneath all the cultural superficialities of race, abilities, and even, dare I say it, gender. I have great respect for people's cultural identities, and in a mystical sense, when I hear somebody say something that is anti-Semitic, I'm suddenly Jewish. When someone says something that's anti-Asian, I'm suddenly Asian. If somebody says something that is ablist, suddenly I'm differently abled. I feel that I am all of these things. Every one of us is all of these things. That is why I feel this pain when anybody is abused. As I said in *Cultural Etiquette,* I think our ultimate challenge and our ultimate goal is to love and nurture one another and all things in creation.

When I was learning about African cultures and herstory, particularly African spirituality, my whole world view began to shift. I began to get disentangled from the Western way of seeing things, and to understand that Western society has compartmentalized everything to death, sometimes even literally. In all traditional societies, everything was originally perceived as a whole rather than compartmentalized. Spirituality was not separated out from agriculture or from science or from the emotions. Everything was interconnected, a single piece.

So, as I tried to reclaim the cultural identities that were interrupted by Western culture, part of that process involved finding out what fits in now, so that I could figure out what would be a good way to be in the future.

When I read herstory, it is as though the old women's voices come alive to me. This is particularly true of the herstory that has been hidden. The reason these things have been hidden is because of the way that spirituality was connected to everything else. Part of the way the boys got the power and continue to keep the power is that they keep us disconnected from the different parts of ourselves. If we women were more connected to the spiritual part of ourselves, we would be uncontrollable.

Also, I feel that lesbianism is often a spiritual calling, not just a sexual orientation. We are often in the forefront of many social changes, sometimes in quiet ways. I see lesbians having a large commitment for change; the percentage of lesbians working for change within the world community is extremely high. That is because it is frequently part of our spiritual calling to be shamans and healers for our cultures. That is why we find ourselves in these roles so much. And that is why we find ourselves in this unique position of providing women's spaces that offer safety and trust.

woman of power: You talked earlier about a shared sense of values and commitment. What are some of the other elements that make up women's community for you?

Three Rivers: In thinking about the elements of women's *culture,* I've noticed that we have our own cuisine. We have dyke cuisine! And it is improving! Years ago, tofu was not nearly as good in dyke homes as I find it to be these days. And this is about more than just food; it's a whole way of taking care of ourselves. Food is part of dyke health care, because women share knowledge about the right kinds of food to eat. Health care, especially diagnosis and cure, is another part of our culture. I find that most of my correct diagnoses and cures come from other women. I notice also that we have our own evolving language and our own politics that are even creeping out into the rest of the world.

Community also means peace and friendship and a feeling of being in relationships with other women where there is trust. Community also means knowing that you can call your sister and that she will come over and help you out. Our house burned down in September of 1991 and the Red Cross helped us out, but what really helped us was what I would call the "Lavender Labrys"! Women from all over the world helped us! Also important in community is the willingness to work things out. When you are in a relationship with somebody, if you have given up on each other, then you don't even argue anymore. But if you are going to stay together and you are committed to both being happy and having an equitable share in the relationship, then you are willing to go through pain and discomfort with each other.

woman of power: You and your partner live in a women's community now. What is that like?

Three Rivers: We don't actually live in a "women's community" per se. Blanche and I live by ourselves in the hills of Appalachia, in Floyd County, Virginia, on one hundred acres of land owned by some dyke friends. There are several women's groups and various unaffiliated individuals in the general area that could loosely be referred to as a community, but we are not part of any sort of intentional community at the moment.

But it is our mutual fantasy to have a community where there is a very large tract of land and where women will have different parts of which they will be caretakers. Women would control their own lives and connect with other women on the land whenever they felt the need to do so.

Being land-based makes a difference because we can control our environment. No one can run us off the land, and we can grow our own food. We can put in our own structures and generate our own power, so that we are less dependent on the larger culture.

When I was living in New York for six years, I really began to miss the sky. I realized then that there are things we need that we can only get from the sky and the land and the trees and the creatures that live there. These are our old connections with the Earth. So part of forming this new women's culture, maybe I should say old/new women's culture, is this reconnection with the Earth, because all traditional cultures have connections with the Earth.

woman of power: How do you think community building can be encouraged among women, especially in a multicultural and multiracial sense?

Three Rivers: I sometimes despair over whether Americans can ever live together in a new way because we bring so many preconceptions with us.

And we don't have very many role models in society to show us the right way to live.

Also, individualism ranks very high in the American value system. A lot of therapy and self-help movements advance attitudes such as, "How does this affect me?" and "I have to take care of myself first." But there is a philosophical difference between saying "I'm not going to let myself be used" and "I'm going to put myself first and foremost, and the hell with you." I think the lack of clarity about these two ideas is one reason why communities are often unsuccessful.

In order to begin to live together, we need to be aware of what we bring with us. We are all burdened with many layers of misinformation, prejudices, and perspectives formed and fed by an "ism"-infested society. We need to continually analyze and dissect all parts of the system of "reality" created by self-serving white, Western thought. This is a lot of work! But it should also be great, exciting fun, because we are intentionally creating something righteous and beautiful from decay and ugliness.

But I would never try to encourage anybody to become the Culture Police. One of the things I have seen some white women who are doing antiracism work get into is a "more antiracist than thou" attitude. They are so cruel to each other! That's not right. We must be patient with one another.

As women, and as women of color especially, one of the things that we have to deal with personally is internalized oppression. We have to struggle with it all the time because we are like salmon going upstream. If we don't constantly go in a different direction than the rest of the culture, then what we have gained is in constant danger of being eroded. Whatever positive feeling I have gained about myself as an African Native American woman, if I don't constantly work on my internalized oppression and stay vigilant, I'll start feeling bad about myself and I'll backslide in a minute. This is because everything I see around me in this place called America, all the images that are directed at me, works to make me feel bad about myself.

Everyone who is working on her own "isms" toward other people also has to stay vigilant and constantly analyze where stuff is coming from. For example, there is much discussion now about cultural appropriation. When women of color say to white women: "This offends us. Please don't do this," I am shocked that white women often argue with us that we shouldn't be offended! I have never understood that. If I'm offended, I'm offended. When I offend someone, it is not my first reaction to tell them

that they have no right to be offended. I try to understand what I am doing to offend them. And if I don't understand, I assume that it is I who is
ignorant, not she. The best thing to do is to have a willingness to do some
work on it. That is something that we are going to need to do if we are to
continue to call ourselves a community.

Sometimes I hear white women asking: "How can we get more women
of color to join our organizations or to come to our concerts?" When
women's groups say that they need more cultural diversity, I understand
that they feel that it's the right thing to do, but when they ask me what
they can do to make it more multicultural, I never know what to say. My
first thought is, well, make it more attractive to women of color. But the
other issue here is that they are making something that they want us to
come to. We need to make things together, to start things up together, not
start something and then ask someone else in after the fact.

This issue is also about friendships and networks. If a couple of friends
who party together and have dinner together think, "Oh, I have an idea,
let's put on this event together" and their friends are multicultural, the
event is inevitably going to be multicultural.

I also think that this question "How can we get more women of color to
join?" can sometimes indicate an artificial construct designed to meet the
needs of white guilt. And as long as that is the focus, then the result is going to be mostly white women and a few faces of color looking bewil-
dered. It is a somewhat new thing to think of the idea of women's community. Most women see "white" when they think of women's
community, and if we are going to have an equitable, multicultural
women's community, then white women will have to give up some
power in whatever way is necessary. This does not mean to give it up totally and be powerless. The idea is for all of us to share equally, however
that can happen, in the power within the community. That means decid-
ing what the values are and what the agendas are and what the organizations are going to be like and where we want to go together.

*women of power: What have you learned from your experiences with an-
tiracism and anticlassism work?*

Three Rivers: The closest I have come to doing any real antiracism work is
giving workshops on the background and cultural perspectives of the
Cultural Etiquette guide, in which I talk about women's herstory. I think
that that gives women some fuel with which to combat racism and internalized oppression. But as far as doing antiracism work directly, I don't,

because I find it too painful. I try to encourage white women to do this work among their sisters.

Herstory is my main interest. I have what African Americans call a "jones," or craving, for herstory. I want women to understand that as Africans and Europeans and Asians, we have a lot of herstory in common. To me, that is the key. The oppression of women by the patriarchal tribes that swept down out of Northern Europe millennia ago coincided with the beginning of some of our oppression as dark-skinned people, too. At one time, we all honored the same deities. I enjoy sharing that knowledge with other women so that we understand the commonalities.

------•◆•------

Excerpts from *Cultural Etiquette: A Guide for the Well-Intentioned*

BY AMOJA THREE RIVERS

Ethnocentrism, according to the *Random House Dictionary of the English Language,* means "a tendency to view alien groups or cultures in terms of one's own" and "the belief in the inherent superiority of one's own group and culture, accompanied by a feeling of contempt for other groups and cultures." It is ethnocentric to use a generic term such as "people" to refer only to white people and then racially label everyone else. This creates and reinforces the assumption that white people are the norm, the real people, and that all others are aberrations, and somehow a bit less than truly human. It is seeing white people as the center and everyone else as variations on the theme.

Within the cultures of many people, more value is placed on relationships, on the maintenance of tradition and spirituality, than on the development and acquisition of machinery. It is ethnocentric and racist to apply words like backward, primitive, uncivilized, savage, barbaric or undeveloped to people whose technology does not include plumbing, microwaves and microchips. Are people somehow more human or more humane if they have more technological toys?

Koreans are not taking over. Neither are Jews. Neither are the Japanese. Neither are West Indians. These are myths put out and maintained by the ones who really have. It is a conscious and time-honored tactic for the white, straight, gentile males at the top to create situations in which the rest of us are encouraged to blame each other for our mutual oppression. Don't fall for it.

Draining the swamps, clearing the forests, taming the West, converting the heathens, manifest destiny, noble, suffering pioneers, intrepid settlers, brave explorers, are all romanticized, idealized, distorted and dishonest images of what was really a prolonged, unconscionably violent invasion and overthrow of many nations of perfectly good people. And it is still going on.

No person of color can be a racist as long as white people maintain power. This is because racism is "power over." A person of color may have race prejudice, but until most of Congress, state, provincial and local governments, the Pentagon, the FBI, CIA, all major industries, the stock exchange, Fortune 500 members, the educational system, health care system, the International Monetary Fund, the armed forces and the police force are all operated and controlled by people of color and their cultural values, we do not have the kind of power that it takes to be racist toward anyone. Similarly "reverse racism" within the context of present society is a contradiction in terms.

The media images we see of poor, miserable, starving, disease-ridden "third world" people of color are distorted and misleading. Nowhere among the tearful appeals for aid do they discuss the conditions that created and continue to create such hopeless poverty. In point of fact, these countries, even after they threw off the stranglehold of colonialism, have been subjected to a constant barrage of resource plundering, political meddling and brutal economic manipulation by European and American interests. Most non-Western countries could function quite adequately and feed themselves quite well if they were permitted political and economic self-determination.

Do not use a Jewish person or person of color to hear your confession of past racist transgressions. If you have offended a particular person, apologize to that person. But don't (please don't) just pick some person of color or Jewish person at random, or who is unrelated to the incident, to confess to and beg forgiveness from. Find a priest or a therapist. Also don't assume that Jews and people of color necessarily want to hear about how prejudiced your Uncle Fred is, no matter how terrible you think he is. It is often painful for us to listen to this type of thing.

Observe how language reflects racism: a black mood, a dark day, a black heart. The meaning of the word denigrate is to demean by darkening. Be creative. There are thousands of adjectives in the English language that do not equate evil with the way people of color look. How about instead of "the pot calling the kettle black" you say, "the pus calling the maggot white"? Think of and use positive dark and black imagery. Dark can be rich and deep and cool and sweet. Black is a sacred color in many religious traditions.

Never, ever, ask any person of color: "Why are you so light-skinned?" "Why is your hair so straight?" "Why is your hair so light?" "Why are your eyes so light?" "Why aren't your eyes slanted?"

Let us face a hard reality: 20th century white society is culturally addicted to exploitation. Cultivate an awareness of your own personal motivations. Do not simply take and consume. If you are white and you find yourself drawn to Native American spirituality, Middle Eastern religion, African drumming, Asian philosophies, or Latin rhythms, make an effort to maintain some kind of balance. Don't just learn the fun and exciting things about us and then go home to your safe, isolated, white, privileged life. Learn about the history of the people whose culture you're dabbling in. Learn how our history relates to your own, how your privilege connects and contributes to our oppression and exploitation. And most importantly, make it a fair exchange—give something back.

Sometimes white people who are drawn to other people's cultures are hungry for a way of life with more depth and meaning than what we find in 20th century Western society. Don't forget that every white person alive today is also descended from tribal peoples. If you are white, don't neglect your own ancient traditions. They are as valid as anybody else's, and the ways of your own ancestors need to be honored, remembered and carried on into the future.

Notes

Condensed from the pamphlet, *Cultural Etiquette: A Guide for the Well-Intentioned,* © 1990 Amoja Three Rivers.

8

Healing Pain and Building Bridges

CHERIE BROWN

———•◆•———

Cherie Brown is the founder and executive director of the National Coalition Building Institute (NCBI), a Washington D.C.–based nonprofit leadership training organization that has launched anti-racism/prejudice-reduction resource teams in forty-five cities worldwide.

Brown has led intergroup conflict-resolution training programs in the United States, Canada, Northern Ireland, South Africa, and the Middle East. She has worked with a wide range of groups, including the NGO Women's Conference in China, the National Organization for Women (NOW), the Los Angeles Police Department, the U.S. Congress, the Council on Foundations, and the National League of Cities.

The author of *The Art of Coalition Building: A Guide for Community Leaders*, she is also the creator of two award-winning videos, "Working It Out: Kids and Race" and "Working It Out: Blacks and Jews on the College Campus."

———•◆•———

woman of power: How would you say your work is related to the theme of "Women in Community"?

Cherie Brown: The National Coalition Building Institute (NCBI) is a non-profit leadership training organization that I founded in 1984. We train community leaders to lead programs that are alternately called "Welcoming Diversity," "Prejudice Reduction," or "Anti-Oppression." Our purpose is to train leaders from diverse organizations who then identify other impactful or powerful leaders in their communities and teach them how to reduce racism, sexism, homophobia, and tough intergroup conflict. We now have chapters in twenty-five cities where we build teams of community leaders who lead this work in their communities. Our leaders include grassroots activists and people who are involved with various constituency-based groups.

All of our programs address issues of sexism and gender, and we have done work for many women's organizations including the National Organization for Women and the International Women's Alliance.

People take the skills they learn in our workshops, form together into a multicultural team, and apply these skills in their own communities. All of our work is basically "train-the-trainer" work, whether it is in public schools where we train young children to lead prejudice reduction work with other children, or in the community where we build a team that in turn leads prejudice reduction work in their community.

One of the important effects of such leadership training is that people learn to have greater influence, reaching out to train people in positions of power and influence, who in turn take these skills and use them to develop more progressive policies and organizations.

woman of power: How does someone distinguish between real conflicts that are in need of being addressed, such as racism, homophobia, or intergroup conflicts, and conflicts that are simply infighting or personal in nature?

Brown: You can err on either end. You can err on the side of stressing only differences, such as "I'm lesbian and you are heterosexual," or "I am white and you are Black" and then see everything you say or do as related to that difference. Or you can very strongly err on the side of not taking differences into account. The way I think about this is that we are shaped by the groups to which we belong, such as class background, race, religion or ethnicity. Any time there is trouble between two women, or between groups of women, those group identities are involved. It is true that we have far more in common with one another than we have differences. But as long as these differences have been used to divide us from one another, we need to look at those differences.

To understand someone that you are having difficulty with, it is helpful to understand their class background, sexual orientation, race, ethnicity, religion, and the many different group identities that are critical to an understanding of what is getting hard, or impeding the relationship, between you and that person. Power dynamics are also important, in terms of which groups have historically oppressed other groups.

woman of power: Your work encourages people to work in coalitions despite a high degree of conflict. How do you foster a positive attitude toward conflict?

Brown: We do training sessions on intergroup conflict resolution skills as well as prejudice reduction. Our experience is that, when people come together to work, it is not just the overt attitudes of bigotry that get in the way; there are also differences in values and beliefs, and often there are very strong emotions attached to these beliefs. So we need several tools. First, we need a process for emotional healing when there are conflicts that include strong emotions, because we can't easily separate out emotions from a conflict, particularly when we are a party to the conflict. The second thing we need is to teach bridge-building skills in an ongoing systematic way. We teach a process in which a group votes on a very tough controversial issue on which they have strong disagreements, and they learn a process for reframing the issue and building bridges.

woman of power: What do you consider the principal barriers to community in the women's community?

Brown: There is a mechanism called "internalized oppression" whereby a group internalizes the mistreatment, the hurtful stereotypes, and the messages that society has about them. Groups sometimes end up believing these negative stereotypes about themselves or other members of their own group. Because each group's oppression is different, the internalized oppression will function differently in different groups.

In some women's organizations, as a result of women having been treated so badly by hierarchies, or by men in authority, the group members understandably have a negative reaction to having authority-based leadership. A negative reaction to authority, however, gets translated into having a negative reaction to any kind of leadership. Some women's groups don't want any women leading. Yet group cohesiveness requires leadership. Whenever a woman attempts to lead in these groups, she gets torn down very quickly by other women who say that she is not doing it right.

I think that a key factor for women who are working in coalition with other women and other groups is to be able to cheer each other on to take leadership. Any time we cheer another woman leader, we are going against our oppression as women and going against the claim that women can't lead the world. Women will emerge with creative leadership, but in order to do that we will also have to do enough of our own healing to be prepared.

A woman in leadership should not put herself out alone and isolated to get attacked. She needs to know how to build support around her so that she is not alone in moving her organization forward. It is critical for women to learn how to interrupt attacks against their leadership.

There is a phenomenon that I call "leadership oppression," namely, targeting leaders, holding them to impossible standards, and then leaving them in isolation. A process we use to increase support for leaders is called "self-estimation." A leader first identifies her strengths in leading the group and then adds the areas that need improvement. Other members contribute additional strengths and areas for improvement. The key part of the self-estimation process is that each member adds what she personally will do to assist that woman leader.

woman of power: Can you explain further what you mean by "leadership oppression?"

Brown: Because women have been so exploited by authoritative leadership, we sometimes respond to that experience by not wanting to be leaders and not wanting to have any leaders. So what often happens when somebody leads is that they are "pedestaled," or put on a pedestal, and then "trashed," or attacked. The reason very few people want to run for elected office in this country is because they run a high risk of getting trashed. The public looks for the weakness in candidates. This is oppression directed toward people who desire to take a leadership role. They are put out there in public in complete isolation, pedestaled, and then attacked. They are never offered any real help when they encounter difficulties.

Leadership attacks are never warranted. An attack is never warranted, because "warranted" usually means that the leader deserves to be attacked. If we are going to support a woman's leadership, then we have to back her solidly. We have to assume that every woman is doing the very best she can (no one intends to be ineffective, incompetent, and so on) so that if someone is doing something that we don't like, we have to figure out how to give her a hand. Attacks usually arise out of a sense of powerlessness. Nobody in a leadership role is going to be perfect. Nobody. Every leader will have major difficulties.

If we are in an activity or organization, we need to first decide whose leadership we want to follow. Any human has a right to decide whether they are going to follow a leader or not. Then, assuming that you have decided to back the overall integrity and policies of a particular woman leader, when she does things that you don't like, then attacking her, or being critical of her, or withdrawing from her is not going to help.

The most effective action is to assume that she is doing the best she can. So if a leader is acting in ways that don't make sense, consider that it may also be your own issues that you need to work out. But if it is not your issues, you still have to think about that other person and help her. We can't just be critical of our leaders and expect these leaders to somehow be effective or begin to change on their own, in isolation, and without any support. When people don't like something, the best approach is for them to figure out a way to change it, and to support the leader at the same time.

When women witness attacks against other women, they are often confused about who to support because they feel that they should support the person who feels powerless. So everybody rallies behind the one who is doing the attacking and supports her and then there is a lot of confusion. In my experience in running groups, somebody will complain about something and then everyone else will join in with their complaints. The group members hold an attitude: "We have to listen to everything everyone thinks and feels, no matter how negative." And what is said under the guise of "honest" feelings is almost always negative. It is rarely encouraging or supportive. When someone starts being negative, even if the group doesn't like what someone is saying, the group is afraid to stop that person. And this endless permissiveness with negativity can be very defeating.

There's a difference between thoughtfully figuring out what piece of information needs to be communicated to a leader to move an effort forward, and merely encouraging and rehearsing negativity.

woman of power: How can we validate someone's position without validating the way she is communicating that position?

Brown: I may be very angry that oppressive things go on, but I also want to be able to change those things. Merely venting anger in a nondirected way is not enough. You can take that anger and turn it into activism, defeating a political candidate or organizing people to take action. We have a right to our anger, but it still needs to be healed. Oppression is unfair, but simply rehearsing anger will not make the real changes in the world that are necessary.

woman of power: I assume that you work frequently with groups in which there are well-entrenched differences. How do you build trust so quickly?

Brown: We have put many years into building models that are nonconfrontational and deeply supportive of people's struggles with each other. All of our trainers are trained to build that kind of safety fairly quickly. Our success has to do with creating models that are not blaming or moralizing, that reduce guilt and moral self-righteousness, and that really try to get in and support all sides.

We also encourage people to tell their personal stories of discrimination and mistreatment. These stories are often emotional, and they touch people's hearts and open us up to our compassion. This is a very powerful way to assist women to see the pain and the struggle beneath the position with which they don't agree.

Our experience is that bridging happens much more quickly when you share these kinds of emotional stories. That is when real healing can take place.

woman of power: Do you think that the consciousness raising that women did in the seventies provided that kind of emotional sharing? Could something like that be reintroduced?

Brown: I think that the kind of internalized oppression work and personal story sharing that I mentioned earlier is part of what went on in early consciousness-raising groups. The claim that is being made by parts of the media that the women's movement has already achieved its major goals, and that, therefore, there is no need for a strong women's movement or continued consciousness-raising efforts, needs to be challenged. There are many issues, from pay equity and child care to parental leave and sexual harassment, that need to be recognized as key women's issues by large numbers of women.

But I also think that we can't separate out the recent attacks on the women's movement that make group-building and cohesiveness difficult from what is currently going on politically as a whole in the United States. There has been a systematic attack on feminism and the women's movement, but there was also a systematic attack on affirmative action for people of color and the whole civil-rights agenda. We have also seen the rise of the Right and the attack on multiculturalism (at times based on trumped-up charges of political correctness) on college campuses. During the Reagan and Bush administrations, the Right has been very successful in misleading some people about what is really going on, and the whole progressive movement has had a hard time pulling itself together and identifying leaders.

Within that process of retrenchment, the women's movement has had its own struggles, but anything less than looking at the whole would be blaming women. So it is not only that women alone need to do consciousness raising. We need a reassertion of a commitment to a very strong women's movement and a very strong civil-rights movement, and these movements need to work side by side.

woman of power: How might this happen?

Brown: There are a lot of people out there who are finding that their lives are hurting, and they are beginning to wake up. They were put to sleep by Reagan and Bush for eleven years and have been kept asleep on all kinds of levels. People are waking up to the fact that the government solutions are not working and that our country is in real trouble. As their lives become harder and harder, they see the need to talk about real options and different ways of doing things, which then connects them to people who are organizing and doing consciousness raising and moving forward. It took many years for the depths of the economic crisis to emerge, and for people to start realizing that they don't any longer have a right to things that they just took for granted. As the myth of meritocracy (that if you just work hard, you'll succeed) hits more and more women, there will be new opportunities to reach out to women with a program that includes issues of social justice for all peoples.

woman of power: Will adversity alone unite us?

Brown: When people are hurting, there are two things that can happen politically. With things as bad as they are now, we have the option of moving toward fascism or else moving toward a progressive agenda. It can go either way.

It requires very good leadership to move people forward in ways that will be useful. At a time when people are hurting as strongly as they are hurting now, we have both incredible dangers and incredible opportunities. That is why NCBI is so committed to the idea of training leaders. Women leaders will need to learn how to handle attacks, and mobilize people on the basis of hope, inspiration, and correct information, not painful emotion. We need to train leaders how to reduce intergroup polarization and build support for courageous position-taking.

A great deal of individual leadership and initiative is required. Collective activity doesn't usually work because every activity needs somebody to be in charge who can take individual initiative, put forward a program, and move the group forward. Part of the role of a leader is to make sure that everybody is listened to and gets equal space. There are many skills that go into being a good leader. These include taking everyone's thinking into account, being willing to admit mistakes, and then learning how to correct the mistakes. At NCBI, we try to address these skills, as well as the skills of bridge building, peace making, and emotional healing for leadership blocks.

We are developing a new program called "Reclaiming Courage toward Principled Leadership." Its purpose is to train public policy officials to build support for taking courageous stands. Women were devastated during the Clarence Thomas/Anita Hill hearings. It was extremely painful to see our public leaders act with so little courage, independence, or principle on behalf of women's issues. Now is a crucial time to train women leaders to mobilize other women to speak out and become leaders themselves. We need to train many women to be leaders who have the skills to build more effective working coalitions, to work through the internalized oppression that keeps women divided, to claim courage, to speak out when that is needed, and to build allies. In order to gain power, we need to choose winnable battles that build trust and confidence between leaders as a way of building a base of power to take on larger issues. Some of the bridge-building issues for women might be family issues like child care or parental leave.

woman of power: In The Art of Coalition Building: A Guide for Community Leaders, *you said that hurt or mistreatment always precedes prejudice.*[1] *Would you elaborate on that idea?*

Brown: I believe that humans are born basically good and cooperative. I don't think it is inherent in our nature to have prejudice. A lot of powerlessness is experienced very, very early in life, and is carried into adulthood. Children are mistreated while very young and are made to do many things that they don't want to do. This mistreatment, or "adultism," is a very pervasive and systemic form of mistreatment affecting most children. Children are lied to and given misinformation about the world. When we are not exposed to an objective picture of reality, and when we don't grow up close to all kinds of people, we end up with a narrow view of the world, and then we are less able to think accurately and function well as adults.

woman of power: How can political groups provide for healing and still accomplish their goals? Is it an ongoing process?

Brown: NCBI teams meet once a month in their own cities, work on their own healing, and get support for leading anti-oppression work. The members of the team have an action-based program to lead in their community, and they have a place to come back to and talk about what went well and where things got hard.

If you don't do ongoing emotional healing work, your leadership will be limited. We all need regular times to do that kind of healing work, perhaps once a month or several times a month, so that the political work we are trying to do is more effective. We teach a specific methodology of healing that helps people to reduce the negative feelings that are preventing them from being effective leaders.

woman of power: You make a distinction between listening to someone else and agreeing with them. Would you elaborate upon that distinction?

Brown: When you listen, you give someone a chance to articulate the hurt underneath their rigid position. This facilitates healing and the person can then think better. And when someone can think better, they are more open to new information. You can't give someone new information when they are upset and expect it to be well received. Listening is a powerful first-stage intervention strategy.

woman of power: In your workshops, you begin with a period where participants spend time with their own group (based on ethnicity, class, sexual preference, and so on) before joining the larger group. How might that strategy apply to the women's movement, by coming together for short-term, ad hoc coalitions and sometimes taking time out for a period of days or months or years to address each group's issues?

Brown: I don't think you can think about it as "take a couple of years." The world is moving too fast. We need to think about it as a simultaneous, parallel process that organizations can undertake. A lot of women's organizations are afraid to develop strong subgroup caucuses. They think, "Well, if the women of color want to meet, then the lesbians will want to meet, and then other groups will want to meet." They are afraid that acknowledging these differences will divide the whole group effort. This is an understandable but misplaced fear. Every group needs to welcome subgroup caucusing. As subgroup members meet, build safety, fall in love with members of their own group, and fight through their own internalized oppression, they are *more* available, not less, to build unity with the larger organization. At the same time, the leaders of each constituency group need to encourage their own subgroup members to claim the agenda of the whole organization as their own, not to get lost in isolation, and to bring their newly gained strength back into the larger organization.

woman of power: What are your thoughts on the prospect of community building in the next decade?

Brown: We will move forward. We are already moving forward. How long it is going to take is hard to tell. We can't tell which way the 1992 U.S. presidential election is going to turn. I think that with the increase of racism, sexism, and other oppressions in this country, we are at a critical point. We will eventually win over a progressive agenda, but it is a question of how long it will take and how much pain and hurt people will have to go through before we arrive at a more just society. There are incredible opportunities right now, but they must be seized.

woman of power: What steps would you like to see taken by the women's movement to incorporate the progressive agenda?

Brown: I would like to see us work on internalized oppression and build alliances with other groups, not just women's groups. I would also like to see women stand up effectively with relaxed confidence against the attacks on the women's movement.

I think a central issue is, "What is real power?" Real power is being able to change somebody. Sometimes being very firm or yelling stops something and sometimes it doesn't. It is not a question of being middle class and polite, it is a question of being effective and powerful. There are a lot of people who run around rehearsing anger at each other who think that they are being powerful when all that is happening is a lot of powerlessness with angry words. Having real power means being able to make things right.

There are times that you have to walk out on somebody; there are times when you have to be very fierce. So my goal is for people to have a repertoire of skills. There is a very clear distinction between having a place to vent the anger and upset and what we do to end this mistreatment. At NCBI, we teach a dual process. People need a place to vent how hurt and angry they are, but they also then need to act. If we are hooked by someone, we are not able to be powerful. We have to get unhooked. We have to be able to vent and heal what is going on for us so that we can move a situation forward.

woman of power: What empowers you to do the work that you do?

Brown: I have had a fierce commitment to ending mistreatment and social injustice since I was very young. Coming out of a Jewish tradition, I gained a strong commitment to social justice issues. The women in my family modeled an enormous amount of strength for me, and I saw a vision of Jewish women being committed to these issues.

Building NCBI has also been an extremely empowering experience. I have a team of thirty leaders all over the world who are deeply committed to me, to one another, and to working together to end injustice. Their loyalty to each other and to the work of NCBI breaks my own isolation and empowers me to keep leading the work.

The National Coalition Building Institute (NCBI)

The National Coalition Building Institute was founded in 1984 by Cherie Brown, whose work in NCBI developed out of twenty years of coalition-building efforts between Blacks and Jews and Arabs and Jews. Her goal in building NCBI was to develop an organization that would integrate the multicultural commitments of political activists with the skills of dispute resolution practitioners, strengthened by an awareness of the importance of emotional healing to reduce imbedded prejudices and intergroup tensions. Cherie has pulled together a unique team of thirty national associates from around the world.

The NCBI associates are Buddhist, Catholic, Jewish, Mennonite, Muslim, Protestant, African-American, Arab, Asian-American, Canadian, Cuban-American, English, Mexican-American, Puerto Rican, white-ethnic, lesbian, gay, and heterosexual. The associates meet together twice a year for three days of intensive training and community building, using the NCBI methodologies of healing to further their own leadership effectiveness as a team.

NCBI has a growing commitment to the concept that every group in society needs to be for every other group. At every NCBI associates meeting, a new group issue is explored in depth to better an understanding of the alliance needs of that particular group and to further NCBI's commitment to ending the society's mistreatment of that group.

The NCBI Mission

The National Coalition Building Institute is dedicated to the development of a new kind of leader, one who values diversity, takes principled stands, and initiates intergroup cooperation. NCBI trains community leaders in every field in the skills of prejudice reduction, intergroup conflict resolution, and coalition building.

NCBI programs emphasize a "train-the-trainer" approach whereby every NCBI-trained leader, from a fifth grader in elementary school to an elected official in the federal government, is taught how to replicate a set of learned skills and thereby train and empower others.

NCBI on the College Campus

Since 1984, NCBI has worked on over one hundred college campuses in North America. NCBI's college and university work has grown dramatically in the last few years in the aftermath of increased racial incidents on campuses. NCBI is one of the few organizations that has offered universities a systemic approach to welcoming diversity and dealing with bigotry. NCBI's work with colleges and universities is broader than one-shot workshops, which can be limited in their effect. Instead, NCBI works with staff, faculty, and students to provide an institutional response to racism. This is accomplished by recruiting and training a campus team of student leaders, administrators, and faculty who act as ongoing trainers and intervenors on campus, leading the prejudice reduction workshop and conflict resolution programs for every department and student group. Following an initial three-day, train-the-trainer program, the campus team becomes an NCBI affiliate and receives ongoing support and consultation from the NCBI staff.

NCBI Chapters

NCBI trains thirty to forty community leaders in each city over a three-day period to lead the prejudice reduction workshop and intergroup conflict resolution models. Following this training, these leaders form an NCBI chapter and work together in teams to lead prejudice reduction programs in local public schools, churches and synagogues, community groups, police and fire departments, unions, businesses and government agencies. NCBI teams also intervene when there are tough intergroup conflicts in the community, teaching effective conflict resolution strategies. One of the unique features of the program is our emphasis on building multicultural teams in each city. Each team works together to lead prejudice reduction programs in their city. In addition, the team meets monthly and is led by a designated local leader who receives additional training and support from NCBI. Many of these teams are affiliated with a local government body such as a city council office or office of human relations. At these meetings, team members learn about each other's cultures and use the NCBI methodologies of healing to help one another to eliminate their own barriers to effective leadership.

NCBI Leadership Seminars

Prejudice Reduction Leadership Seminar

This seminar teaches participants all the steps involved in developing and leading prejudice reduction workshops and diversity programs. This workshop teaches participants how to heal the emotional and institutional impact of discrimination and to remove the hurt, misinformation, and powerlessness that keep racism, sexism, anti-Semitism, homophobia, and other forms of discrimination in place. Participants learn how to lead workshops that welcome diversity, unfreeze prejudicial attitudes, and interrupt oppressive remarks and actions. Specific tools are taught that empower individuals to be constructive allies on behalf of other groups.

Leadership Training Seminar

This seminar teaches participants the many different skills that are necessary for providing influential leadership in ending discrimination, reducing intergroup conflict, and building multigroup coalitions. Participants learn to reduce tough intergroup tensions, locate the underlying issue in any complex conflict situation, and reframe politicized controversial issues in a way that builds bridges. They learn to use specific tools for building alliances across group lines. Participants are assisted in the process of reclaiming their own individual leadership abilities and healing the harmful effects of powerlessness and mistreatment that can inhibit powerful coalition-building leadership.

Notes

1. See Cherie Brown, *The Art of Coalition Building: A Guide for Community Leaders* (Philadelphia: The American Jewish Committee, 1984).

9

Meeting Us Halfway

CAROLE POPE

———•◆•———

Carole Pope was the founder and executive director of Our New Beginnings, a nonprofit sentencing alternative for female offenders in Portland, Oregon. Our New Beginnings was housed in a 44-room Victorian house where the women were called "clients" rather than "inmates" and were able to keep their children with them. The recidivism rate at Our New Beginnings was estimated to be 30 to 35 percent lower than that of other programs, and the success rate was about 65 percent.

———•◆•———

The Community of "Our New Beginnings"

woman of power: When did you first become interested in creating Our New Beginnings?

Carole Pope: The idea to create Our New Beginnings came to me while I was serving time as an inmate in the Oregon Women's Correctional Center, from 1977 to 1981. I have a master's degree in music and I came from an upper-middle class family, but on the flip side, I was raised by alcoholics, was abused as a child, and became an alcoholic myself at age seven. I was paroled after serving twenty-one months, but I found that no one would hire me because I was an ex-con, so I stopped cooperating with the parole board and was sent back to prison. That was when I began talking with other inmates about our shared experiences of sexual and physical abuse, and eight of us began to talk about how there was a need for a program that would help us to break the cycle of abuse and incarceration, a place to heal.

There was a real need for a program where women could turn their lives around. Women have always been the invisible part of the prison system because there are fewer women in the system. Residential programs for women did not exist at that time in Oregon, and I realized that there were hundreds of women just like me who needed help to make the transition. The corrections system does not help women to function in society; in fact, it increases their feelings of worthlessness and does nothing to prepare them for living outside. Prisons don't spend time or money treating the problems that got women there. I saw some women return to prison within twenty-four hours.

I began to study in the prison law library (which we got through a lawsuit) and became the first woman inmate in Oregon to be certified as a paralegal. Then, when I got out in 1981, I got a job with an attorney and began helping other ex-inmates in any way I could by referring them to social service agencies or finding them a place to live or getting them a bus ticket. By 1982, my efforts paid off when I began to be recognized by the corrections community and received some grants; and by 1986 the program received some national media attention and I was able to hire staff and move into this house. But this program runs on a deficit and many times I have gone without a salary, even for as long as ten months. The name of the program is taken from a jazz album by Morgana King. She had been in a terrible car accident and they said that she would never sing again, so she called it "Our New Beginnings."

woman of power: How do you build a sense of community in your program?

Pope: In order to have a community of women like this, you have to build trust. I have a unique way of dealing with people. I trust them absolutely and I haven't been disappointed very often. I trust these women until they show me that I can't. The majority of the programs don't trust them from the beginning, and in prison they assume that you are a liar. But it never dawned on me not to trust these women. I am very aware of their potential, and when you trust them and give them that humanity and dignity, they rise to the occasion.

I have, of course, worked with women who screwed up and used drugs, and I'm the first one to send them back to prison because they are not amenable to treatment. Not everyone can live outside of prison, but those who can flourish should be allowed to. If someone commits a crime and pays their dues, they shouldn't have to start at the bottom of the ladder, and I think society needs to recognize that.

When women make up their minds to change, when they are finally ready to change, they will. But you have to be there to help them, or they may not try again. Women ex-offenders have a right to put their lives back together, and the women's community needs to be there for them. They have to learn how to love themselves. We have to teach them things that should have been taught to them by their parents but never were, like how to trust. Rehabilitation is also inner-child work. These women need to believe in themselves and to learn what led them to where they are now. They need to learn to accept love and help, and to learn accountability and responsibility.

Ninety-eight percent of the women I work with are victims of incest, and ninety percent have been substance abusers for eleven years or more. They don't care about themselves. Society has to take responsibility for that. These women feel worthless. They have prostituted themselves for drugs and gone through incredible pain and they don't care about themselves at all. I care about them, and yet their immediate response is to assume you are running some kind of a scam. The reality is that if you consistently show them that you care and keep giving them back their dignity and their humanity, many of them will begin to heal. It takes a long time to begin the recovery process. When the pain is too great, you still need to cover up the pain until you are in a place where you are safe enough to let go of it. And this place is a place where they can do it. This place is a home.

We treat every woman as an individual with individual needs, and if we don't have a program to suit her, we create one if we can afford it. They need role models and we are able to give them role models by having a diverse staff. For example, one member of my staff is a former heroin addict in recovery; she was an addict for thirty years so women who have a heroin history see what she has achieved. She is a role model for them and they know that they can do it too.

These women need jobs and places to live. No one will rent to them because they don't have credit. No one wants "those people" living next door, but the reality is that those people already live next door. People don't want to hire them because they are ex-cons. I have women with AIDS who aren't allowed into some of the hospices because they are IV-drug users. No one wants to deal with them.

woman of power: What was the response of the women's community to your program?

Pope: I thought women in the women's community would be some of the strongest supporters of these women and that they would be the first to raise the banner for the issues of ex-offenders. What a disappointment that was! When I got out of prison, the lesbian community often didn't want to deal with me because I represented the offender part of their community. There are lesbian women in my program who need role models, but the community treats the situation as one of "us" and "them." They see offenders and ex-offenders as "those people." The lesbian and the feminist communities have quite often been unwilling to reach out and share the responsibility for helping these women to heal.

Society needs to look in the mirror. It also needs to understand that although women in prison are responsible for their actions, they are only responsible up until the point that they are truly culpable. When they have been abused as children, someone else also must share the responsibility. And society won't do it. Society's answer to this problem is out of sight, out of mind—the attitude is to lock them up and throw the key away.

Recognizing that we have issues in common like childhood physical and sexual abuse will open up the area of commonality. There is very little difference, if any, between "us" and "them." If we are going to build bridges between the communities, we have to admit that there is a problem. My women need to take fifty percent of the responsibility because they are responsible for their actions. People in society at large, who have shown their apathy and their inability or unwillingness to deal with abuse and incest and other problems, need to begin to take responsibility. The women I work with seem to be becoming a class of people to be annihilated. That is unacceptable to me.

I trust in these women and I believe in them. One thing I did to overcome the obstacles in my own life was to stop drinking. I will be sober ten years this year. I also got angry, because I decided that I was not going to be abused anymore and I was not going to be forced to live on the outside looking in. I refused to do it. I didn't demand a lot; I said, "Just respect me and give me my chance; and if I screw up, I'll take my licks." That's all these women need, a chance to change their lives.

We give them the tools they need to do it: parenting skills, twelve-step programs to deal with addictions, child care, counseling, medical help, education, the skills to help themselves. It is a place of rebirthing, a place to break the cycle of abuse. We empower the women to do it, so that they don't have to go back out and make the same choices. It makes me angry when a woman can document twenty-five years of battering with the police department, kills the man who battered her, and immediately is called the perpetrator. Feminist legal skills have successfully redefined killing a batterer as self-defense, so some good work *has* been done. But the women's community needs to get more involved.

I think society has created a fearful image of offenders, so we build prisons and cages in which to put these women, instead of looking at them for who they are. I think that if we are going to build trust, the women in the women's community have to give fifty percent and meet us halfway, and then my women will give the other half. My women do go halfway. They go out into the world to learn to trust. They are willing to do it, and they get frustrated. I just want the women's community to be willing to come halfway. That is all I have ever asked.

10

An Honorable Ethic

ANDREA DWORKIN

Andrea Dworkin's radical-feminist critique of pornography and sadomasochism began with her first book, *Woman Hating*, published in 1974 when she was twenty-seven. She went on to speak often about the harms to women of pornography and addressed the historic rally in 1978 when 3,000 women attending the first feminist conference on pornography, held the first Take Back the Night March, and shut down San Francisco's pornography district for one night.

In 1980, Andrea read *Ordeal* by "Linda Lovelace" Marchiano and "understood from it that every civil right protected by law in this country had been broken on Linda's prostituted body."[1] Andrea then asked Yale law professor Catharine A. MacKinnon for help in bringing a civil-rights suit in Linda's behalf—a legal idea that had never been tested. In Linda's case, they found, the statute of limitations had expired; but *Deep Throat*, the product of her abuse, was still for sale. In effect, this ongoing violation of Linda's civil rights was protected by law.

While coteaching a course on pornography at the University of Minnesota Law School in 1983, Dworkin and MacKinnon were commissioned by the Minneapolis City Council to draft a local ordinance that would embody the legal principle, first proposed by Andrea in Linda's behalf, that pornography violates the civil rights of women. Dworkin, MacKinnon, and others organized public hearings on the ordinance—the first time in history that victims of pornography testified directly before a governmental body.[2]

The civil-rights antipornography ordinance was passed by the city councils of Minneapolis and Indianapolis and by referendum (with 62 percent of the vote) in Bellingham, Washington.[3] Andrea's testimony before the Attorney General's Commission on Pornography in 1986 was acknowledged by several commissioners whose final report unanimously endorsed "legislation affording protection to those individuals whose civil rights have been violated by the production or distribution of pornography."[4]

The Dworkin/MacKinnon ordinance is under consideration in the governments of Sweden, the Philippines, New Zealand, Great Britain, Ireland, Germany, Australia, and other countries; portions of the ordinance have been incorporated into such federal U.S. bills as the Pornography Victims Protection Act and the Pornography Victims Compensation Act; the Dworkin/MacKinnon concept of harm to women as being definitional of pornography was recognized in law by the Canadian Supreme Court; and a revised version of the complete Dworkin/MacKinnon ordinance was introduced into the Massachusetts State Legislature at the end of 1991.

Pornographers had begun to attack Andrea personally long before her civil-rights approach was proposed in law. For instance, *Playboy* had printed insults against her regularly, and *Hustler* published a series of sexual and defamatory cartoons of Andrea and of her mother. After the Dworkin/MacKinnon ordinance was introduced in 1983, however, such attacks on Andrea escalated. *Screw* sexually caricatured her as a cartoon centerfold, and *Penthouse* ran full-page ads equating Andrea with Jerry Falwell and the Ayatollah Khomeini. In April 1987, *Penthouse* published a cover-story interview with Andrea that had been obtained fraudulently by a woman who told Andrea she was writing for an Israeli newspaper. Several self-styled feminists have published personal attacks on Andrea in men's pornography magazines, and a lesbian sadomasochistic pornography magazine has joined them in its frequent sexualized ridicule of her.

Andrea has been stigmatized professionally for her efforts to help women harmed by pornography, in part because U.S. media conglomerates tend to side with pornographers' right to turn women into "speech." As a result, Andrea's options for publishing in this country have dropped off dramatically. Her last three books—the novel *Ice and Fire, Letters from a War Zone,* and the novel *Mercy*—have had to be published in England first, more than a year before a U.S. publisher could be found.

In 1991 the BBC broadcast an hour-long documentary in its Omnibus series called "Against Pornography: The Feminism of Andrea Dworkin." Filmed in New York City and Portland, Oregon, it included interviews with Andrea and her conversations with women of various ethnicities who had been used in prostitution and pornography, most since childhood. It was watched by more viewers in England than any other Omnibus program and is now being syndicated throughout Europe. So far attempts to get this documentary broadcast in the United States have been unsuccessful.

There are many more men who have read the continuing attacks on Andrea in pornography magazines than there are women and men who have actually read her writings or heard her speak. Joining in the attacks on Andrea by pornographers have been scores of recent books by academics, including academic feminists, many of whom take issue with Andrea's radical-feminist views on pornography and sadomasochism, often in terms that originated with pornographers.[5]

In the following interview, Andrea discusses these experiences.

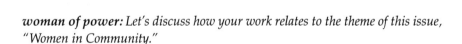

woman of power: Let's discuss how your work relates to the theme of this issue, "Women in Community."

Andrea Dworkin: I think that my work broadens what has been an implicit feminist definition of community. That definition has been unthinkingly middle class and has—not purposefully, but nevertheless effectively—excluded a lot of poor women. Working on issues such as pornography and prostitution brings poor women into the community of political women. It has been a very effective way of expanding the feminist community in the real world. In other words, instead of having an idea of community that is basically restrictive and has to do with an "in" group of people, my work has pushed the boundaries of feminism further out into the world. Rather than bringing women into a kind of privileged safe space, my work is bringing feminism out into the larger world. So I think that there are a lot of women who are included in the feminist community now who were excluded before, and to me that is very, very important.

A lot of things are now being said about women's lives that have never been said before. All kinds of silences have been broken, which I think is partly due to my work, although certainly not to my work alone. The whole idea of bringing the realm of sexual abuse into every discussion about the status and condition of women has helped to break down a lot of the barriers that have kept us from being able to tell the truth and to explore what really happens to women.

woman of power: In many ways your work is seen as radical truth telling, and there have been those who have wanted to silence you because of it. How have your experiences influenced your sense of community?

Dworkin: More and more I ask myself: What does feminism have to do with women? The answers aren't always obvious because the bad ethics in relation to me and my work that have saturated something that calls itself the feminist community have certainly made me an outsider and an exile in that community. And, if at the same time my work means so much to so many women, both inside of the women's movement and outside of it, what does that then say about this self-consciously ghettoized feminist community, the women who are representing the movement to the politicians and the media?

I think it is extraordinary that the way I have been treated has been embraced by the women's community. References to me in the women's press tend to not only be disrespectful; they tend to be caricatures. My name is used symbolically for things that people hate, which is an extraordinary thing to have happen to you. And there hasn't yet been any principled repudiation of that kind of treatment of me and my work.

At my worst moments, I think that if the name-calling, the misrepresentation, and the stigmatizing of me that feminists have been willing to accept really is acceptable to them, then certainly the women's movement isn't a home for me. And also, if lesbian sadomasochism, or dominance and submission in any form, represents the aspirations of feminism, I don't want it to be a home for me. So I think about that and then I think, wait a minute, you're getting your priorities really mixed up here because these really are very few women who are being used for their propaganda value by the media and by the pornographers, and it is all those other women who don't have access to expression who are the women who matter, and they have always been the women who matter to me.

As long as feminism still seems to have at its center something that I regard as an honorable ethic, then I feel I can continue to be part of the women's movement. But if I thought for a minute that the pro-pornography and the advocacy of sadomasochism of some self-proclaimed feminists were the ethic of this movement, I would disassociate myself from it.

woman of power: How do you think we can move beyond those "bad ethics" when they appear in order to create an atmosphere of respect for one another?

Dworkin: I have found the tolerance of these bad ethics extraordinary, especially in view of the fact that this was a movement that, when it erred, tended to err in the other direction. When some of these incredible sexual attacks appeared in writing—very aggressive and violent things written by women—I remember recognizing that this was a way of trying to humiliate women like me and shut us up. But I still believed that women within the women's movement would not be allowed to treat other women like that. I was disabused of that notion because I never saw anyone say to them in print, "Your ethics are not feminist ethics. You can't say those things about other women. You can't say that to other women."

I think that feminists have been afraid that the things that happened to me would happen to them if they became associated with me. That is the triumph of bullies. That happens in many movements—the people who are the most abusive dominate the discourse because others are afraid to stand up to them.

My sense of community these days is with women who are doing things that really confront and attack male sexual exploitation of women. I work with women who are prepared to put themselves on the line, and there are a lot of these really brave women everywhere. In fact, I am surprised to find that I'm treated with a great deal of love and veneration when I travel into women's communities and speak to women's groups.

woman of power: There is a long history of trying to distinguish between trashing and constructive criticism in this community. Have you arrived at any ideas about how to foster constructive criticism as a means to build community?

Dworkin: Well, I certainly know that there is a difference between having disagreements with someone, even if they are serious disagreements that are hurtful, and making another woman's life a target for male aggression and ridicule and humiliation. There's a difference between having respect for someone and treating them without any respect at all. That seems to me to be the fundamental issue. There are ways of having political disagreements that are essentially respectful of the other person's humanity.

Many of these things I am saying apply to the media as well as to individual women in the women's movement. I don't have any sense of community inside the so-called women's media or inside the professional feminist community, because it has become impossible to know what it means when a woman says that she is a feminist. And I don't mean ideologically; I mean ethically what it means.

woman of power: Would you elaborate upon what you mean when you say that the women's movement needs to maintain an "honorable ethic"?

Dworkin: If I may, I would like to talk about it in context, discussing the circumstances within which I have experienced the problems. In other words, I will talk about the choices I have made that I think are honorable ones, so that it doesn't cover the whole spectrum of what ethical behavior is but is at least concrete and understandable. It is easy enough to say, "People should treat each other well," but if they do not, then what do you do?

In terms of what has happened to me, it is very clear, in my view at any rate, that feminists should not attack women by name in ways that are disrespectful. I think it is deeply unethical for women who call themselves feminists to publish specific attacks on other feminists in pornography magazines. And I think that when women see other women being attacked in this way, they should not provide political and social support for the women who are doing the attacking, as if attacks were merely a neutral situation or as if they just don't matter.

I believe strongly in not engaging in public fights with other women or attacking them in the male domain in ways that are humiliating. I think that is really important, and I have refused to do it. There are one or two exceptions where I felt, not always for a noble reason, that I had to defend myself or engage in a public debate. But in general I have refused to accept invitations to engage in highly contentious, adversarial set ups between women. I think it is an ethical principle for feminists that women live in a world that is filled with hostility that is directed towards us, and that we take it as a principle that you do not make the world more hostile by treating women with contempt in public.

woman of power: Have other women accepted engagements to debate you in adversarial settings?

Dworkin: Yes, they have accepted invitations that range from programs such as "The MacNeil/Lehrer News Hour" to television shows that are much more clearly commercial and pandering in nature, to forums in intellectual or political magazines that in fact have nothing to do with ideas and whose intention is to provide the equivalent of women doing mud wrestling. I refuse these invitations because I think of it as really wrong, but other women have been happy to get newspaper coverage. They get their articles published, not just in pornography magazines but in left-wing political magazines and in more commercial venues such as *The Village Voice.* Anybody who writes a really vicious article can get it published. I have experienced the willingness of all kinds of women to say of me to the pornographers, "It is fine if you hurt her." When they, as feminists, are willing to be used in a vicious way to attack me or other women, they break down the barriers that we created to prevent men from attacking women. Because if it is all right for feminists to do it to one another, then it is not so bad for men to do it.

We have to ask why these women are attacking other women and why still other women are tolerating it. I think that internalized self-hatred has a lot to do with the embracing of sadomasochism. Women are after all brought up to experience ourselves as being real only when we're being demeaned, and sadomasochism is the perfect sexual expression for what it means to be a woman who has been taught to hate herself. But I also think that cowardice is involved because nobody is going to get hurt by attacking me. What am I going to do to them? But if you attack the publisher of *Penthouse* or *Hustler,* things happen to you, for instance, the things that have happened to me: I find myself publishing in another country because I can't even publish in the United States anymore; I can't make a living; and the media feel free to ridicule and despise me.

I think that there was a lot more willingness to stand up in the earlier years of the women's movement, partly because women thought that it would be easier than in fact it is. There was also a tremendous sense of solidarity between women that was very much shattered when certain women began taking a propornography stance. There was a sense that they valued their alliances with men more than they cared about the lives of women and that they valued their access to media, careers, and status in society, attained through their alliances with men, more than they valued other women. That created a rift that couldn't even have been foreseen in the early days of the women's movement when repudiating those kinds of benefits from men was really a point of pride.

woman of power: Do you think that techniques such as criticism/self-criticism could be reintroduced into our communities to facilitate better communication?

Dworkin: That is an interesting idea, but what I remember of the use of that kind of mechanism, specifically on the Left and then later in parts of the women's movement, is that it became extremely destructive. People were really torn to pieces because what often happens is that a group gangs up on an individual. In the women's movement, it kind of goes back to the phenomenon of "trashing." That seems to have been more characteristic of the early women's movement in that women who achieved any kind of prominence in their own community could pretty much expect to have this happen to them. That doesn't seem to be the case in the same way now, but that could be because there is not the same sense of community.

woman of power: Do you think that the kind of thing that has occurred during the pornography debates is an extension of the trashing phenomenon?

Dworkin: The pornography debates went to the tremendous weaknesses of feminism. Dealing with the issue of pornography really tells women to "put up or shut up." It doesn't do it purposely. It just means that you have to be prepared to take on this external enemy who is real and powerful and dangerous. You have to be prepared to do it because a lot of women are being hurt. I think that a lot of women were not prepared to do it. They liked feminism when it was easier, and when it had to do with self-affirmation instead of with this particular kind of political struggle. However, while a lot of people think that the pornography issue has divided the women's movement, it is my perception that the divisions are much more basic than any particular issue and that those divisions were there before. For instance, the way the press formulates it is that these are women who agree on everything else but disagree on pornography. In fact we don't agree on everything else. We have very deep differences that are crystallized by this issue because it is dangerous.

woman of power: Does it seem to you that perhaps one of the problems with this issue is that it revealed something to women on a personal level? A lot of women had difficulty seeing this issue in a political light when women insisted that it was a matter of their personal choice or preference.

Dworkin: I think that that is right. I didn't understand at all how women were taking this to be about them personally, because to me it was personal only in the sense that dominance and submission define the world we all live in. It never occurred to me that anybody would address this issue as if they were pure and other people weren't—that was never a starting point. It is not a matter of taking your personal, sexual life and subjecting it to the scrutiny of anybody else's politics. It is much more a matter of understanding that you are part of a process, that you are in a process of change. You are moving from a world in which the dominant ethic is hierarchy and dominance and you want to move into a world of equality. You want to do it in your own life and you want to do it out in the world, and those two things are connected in some way.

I do have a lot of feelings and opinions and knowledge about what the meaning of certain choices or of certain acts is, but I have never put myself in the position of telling anybody how it is that they should live. I did presume that being a feminist meant that you wanted to live with an ethic of equality because that is so much its meaning to me. But that doesn't mean that I thought that on the very day somebody decided to live with equality as their basis, their relationships became immediately equal. Because life isn't like that.

woman of power: If you step back to a time before this furor over pornography began, do you think that we, as a community, could have discussed issues such as these among ourselves, issues such as how to bring one's personal and political beliefs into harmony, without a similar result? Are such issues inevitably difficult?

Dworkin: I think that from the earliest times, feminists tried to have this be a point of discussion long before there was a real politics around pornography and that it always ended up with enormous conflicts. For instance, the first time that it happened in my experience as a feminist was over the issue of lesbian separatism, where issues of how women lived were considered the most important issues. Women were judged, and judged very harshly, on the basis of who their friends were and what their alliances were. That applied to everything from the continuing question of whether you could take your male children with you to a women's event to whether you should publish your book with what was then called a "male" publisher. I think that was a very unsuccessful way of dealing with it.

Clearly the pornography issue has been handled no more successfully. My work always framed these issues very much as a fight against male power. Perhaps these personal issues could have been raised among women, but the operative dynamic has to be empathy if you are going to commit yourself to discussing anybody's personal life. Having other people judge us by knowing such personal things about us makes us extremely vulnerable. And the participation in the conversation has to be voluntary, because not everybody agrees to have their personal life subjected to the scrutiny of other people.

woman of power: You mentioned the positive experience of community you have felt as you travel across the country meeting grassroots or activist women. What contributes to that sense of community? What makes that kind of community possible?

Dworkin: These women are fighting for their lives, and meeting someone on that basis is really different from meeting them through the common ground of ideology or the common ground of lifestyle. My contacts with women are most often on the basis of, "We are in a state of emergency: we can't feed our children," or "We are being beaten," or "We have got to get off the streets," or "We can't do this anymore." What that means is that there isn't any social pretense, and that people have already made the decision that what they need is more important than anything they would try to protect. Most of the women I am close to politically have really hit bottom at some point in their lives. That is also true for me, and that forms a basis in my life for feeling a kind of closeness.

My sense of community has really changed over an issue of violence, the advocacy of sadomasochism in the women's movement. That was a monumental point of transition for me. My sense of community is with disenfranchised, poor women who are fighting for their lives and activist women, most of whom come out of that same group of women, and they care about the ways in which women are exploited and hurt sexually. They are where I come from and they are where I'm going back to. That is where I find home and I believe I could go anywhere in the country and they would always care about me and I would always care about them.

woman of power: Do you foresee a time when women like these will not be marginalized?

Dworkin: I hope that that time is coming. It won't come as long as we have feminists allied with people who hurt women for profit, who are basically consigning women to be destroyed. They are not taking any responsibility to provide the kind of protections that are needed as a consequence of prostitution and pornography and rape. They are not taking responsibility for what it means to protect sadomasochism, what it means to protect pornography, what it means to think that prostitution is a form of liberation for women. That means that all these women who are hurt by these things and used in these ways are consigned not only to being marginal but to being disposable. As long as that is part of the women's movement, I think that the movement's effectiveness is extraordinarily compromised and that its integrity is virtually nonexistent and that we have no moral ground to stand on. I think that we've lost a tremendous amount of credibility because of that.

The women's movement has to be a movement for all women. More and more I see many of our problems as class issues. Many women have a completely revisionist view of what these questions are about, as if prostitution is just another middle-class lifestyle choice, which it isn't. That view is almost contemptuous of any kind of reality. It has no comprehension in it of what it is like to be poor, to be without recourse. It is the most extraordinary identification with male power. If prostitution had been empowering for women, we women would now be empowered.

woman of power: Do you think that this problem of interpretation stems from the fact that some of these women are dealing with prostitution and pornography as academic issues, at an abstract or theoretical level, rather than actually talking with women who are in or have been employed in these industries?

Dworkin: Although action is not the only way to learn, it is the only way to learn about how male supremacy really functions. A great deal of what I have learned about both pornography and the pornography industry has come from being an activist. You can't make it up in your head; you can't think it through; you have to have the experience of confrontation, because you can't anticipate the way in which institutions that have never been challenged will react when they are challenged. You can't learn it from books; it is not in books. So I think that there's an enormous amount of hubris in believing that thinking is the way to understand how to make women free. Nobody has ever made women free before, so how is it that established theories can tell us what we need to know?

woman of power: How do you address the idea that 1970s feminism was somewhat monolithic and obscured differences?

Dworkin: Concepts like "difference" and "diversity" have been used as another rhetorical way of destroying any political practice that tries to address what happens to women per se. These ideas are never used to cut the other way. For instance, there are many, many kinds of racism, many configurations of racism, but we don't have to talk about "racisms." We can know what we're talking about without creating a whole new jargon to address the fact that white supremacy in the United States is different from anti-Semitism in Europe. There are configurations of racism all over the world that demand our attention, yet that does not invalidate what it means for African Americans to talk about their experiences of racism in the United States.

We are being told that difference is a reason to invalidate many of the perceptions that women have come to about how women are treated as women. I see it as a very reactionary ploy to take people's political attention off of gender. With this kind of theoretical strategy, one takes a concept that is very valid, in this case the idea that women are differently situated in terms of race and class, and then uses that perception not to make the discourse richer but to put a stop to an investigation of gender. The Left has been doing that for a long time and to me this is a very familiar left-wing strategy. I don't see why the inclusion of understanding that women have deeply different experiences as well as deeply similar experiences should stop investigations into what women have in common.

I think it is very important to speak from who you are, and it is very important to comprehend that the experiences of all women have got to be articulated by all women. That is part of the reason that my fight to expand the bounds of the women's movement is such a strong one, to deal with the lives of women who haven't been included. More and more women have to be involved in saying what their situations are and how they see the world. Nobody can do it for somebody else, but I do think there are all kinds of articulations of what women's experience are, about which all kinds of women say, "Yes, that is also true for me."

woman of power: So, you do find the commonalities in your work?

Dworkin: Absolutely. Even though, for instance, I'm the first one who's going to say that I think pornography is playing itself out along class lines, I do see the commonalities. For instance, I think that rape is a close-to-universal female experience and I think that there is something fundamentally the same about what it does and what it is. It does precisely what it is intended to: it breaks a woman into pieces.

woman of power: So, in this sense, what you call the self-conscious or ghettoized feminist community is not necessarily representative of the women you're talking about?

Dworkin: Yes, and I really think that it is such a small number of women who have very little to do with the real world of organizing women. But at the same time they are useful to men in that they become a kind of emblem of the women's movement in the world. They are the women the media use to discredit the rest of us. They are pandering to every male stereotype of what men want feminists to be, and so I see that part of the movement as being incredibly destructive and lacking in self-respect. A real contempt for other women is in effect the dynamic behind their politics.

I think it's really tragic that the many women who don't agree with these women have let them use the women's movement as a platform but the damage has been done. In other words, it has been accepted, it has been tolerated, it is recognizably a part of feminism and that deeply compromises the women's movement.

woman of power: Do you think that some of the silence on the subject is an attempt to be inclusive, not to criticize other women within the movement?

Dworkin: I'm sure that there are good intentions in this tolerance. I think that there is a desire not to trash other women and not to be judgmental and I can only say that I share that. For instance, I'm talking with you about principles, I'm not trashing individuals. I certainly share those values of not wanting to insult and hurt other women. In my view, "the other side" is not these women but men in power.

Every time that these women come forward into the public arena to hurt other women, they present themselves as the other side. Now, why they want to stand in for the other side I don't know, but they keep insisting this is an argument among feminists. I think that this is a struggle of women against male power. And I refuse to accept it as an argument among feminists. In my opinion, they refuse to see the extraordinary propaganda value of what they're doing for men who are hurting women.

So whatever the good intentions of women who remain silent on this subject, other women who identify themselves as feminists are acting as the defenders and protectors of pornography every single day in this country. Nothing has happened in the women's community to say that they do not represent feminism. We have had ten years of this.

woman of power: You said that you have seen many grassroots and activist women who are doing community building in the U.S. Are you encouraged that this work can continue under perhaps a different name than feminism?

Dworkin: You know, we're certainly all still calling it feminism and our view is that we're part of the best of this movement, not the worst of it. I do believe that communities of women fighting for the dignity of women and resisting male oppression are growing in this country. I see a tremendous split between what is happening on the grassroots level and what the women's movement as a self-conscious entity represents. I don't think that they are the same thing at all.

There is an extraordinary break between the women who are real grassroots feminists in this country and the women who are representing the women's movement to politicians and the media. My future is with women whose lives have to do with rescuing other women and with fighting against male exploitation of women. What I'm saying is schematic; it is not intended as a condemnation of all the women in one place and an idealization of all the women in the other place.

The problem, and I think it should be considered a political problem, is why doesn't the grassroots level have any meaning to this entity called the women's movement? I don't see any real bridges between the professional women's movement and the many activists I meet when I travel and all the women who may not call themselves feminists, but whose lives have in fact been transformed by feminism and who would like to move closer to the women's movement but who don't trust it to be a safe place for them. And I, of all people, can't tell them they are wrong, so I feel totally paralyzed on that point.

It is sometimes said that feminists view women as victims, but the issue has never has been one of victimization; it has always been one of oppression. That is a very American rendering of what the problem is in the sense that it basically psychologizes the problem and says that is a matter of your attitude towards these events, not a matter of these actual events. My view is that feminism is a matter of what is actually happening to women. A system of oppression exists that keeps women powerless relative to men. It ensures that women remain targets for sexual violence and establishes the domination of women as normal. We are fighting that concept of normalcy.

We do not see women as victims and neither did women in the 1970s. If anything, 1970s feminists saw women as people who could easily triumph over these political conditions. And, as I suggested earlier, a lot of the divisions within the women's movement probably came about because it is not easy to triumph over these conditions. It requires sustained political struggle, probably through your whole lifetime, maybe through the next generation's lifetime. Once it became clear that it wasn't going to be an easy victory, a whole lot of women arrived at another kind of accommodation with reality.

I think the worst political problem we face is that we're a population who has been widely sexually abused. No other oppressed group of people deals with that specific reality. I don't know what the answer to it is except to continue organizing around the issue of sexual abuse, to keep sharing what is in effect the pain of doing this work, and hoping that each small success will bring in more women. When women collapse, or burn out, or give up, those things hurt all of us. It's not fair that the people who are the most hurt by our culture are the ones who bear the biggest burden for social change, but there isn't any way around it.

woman of power: What empowers you personally? How do you keep going in spite of the difficulties you have faced?

Dworkin: I take my life day by day and I think that's a good way to do it. I really love writing, and that gives me an enormous amount of happiness and a tremendous sense of well-being. I listen to music and take walks— all kinds of things give me pleasure. I think it is vital to have friends and to try to be good to yourself in some way, but mostly I think survival has more to do with luck.

I also try to take anything that has happened to me in my life and find a way to use it for women. I try to find information in it about male power and how it works, and if you do that, you are not defeated by the painful things that happen because they have value. I feel very lucky to have survived long enough to see that my work has value to some people.

woman of power: What has your experience been in finding your own cultural identity and working with other women from different backgrounds?

Dworkin: My experience has been one of acceptance. I really believe that when a woman speaks I need to listen and learn from her experience, and sometimes I'm really shocked by the blinders I have on. I have tried to use my own ethnic or personal identity as a Jewish woman to think about the things that have a kind of visceral reality for me. I've tried to use it as a base of experience and take it and make it part of how I actively see the world. I think that that goes along with listening to others and accepting them.

woman of power: What are some of your experiences with antiracism and anti-classism work?

Dworkin: Well, I try to embody it in the issues that I'm dealing with. I have tried to make people aware that pornography is one of the main ways in which race hatred is sexualized and perpetuated in this country. I have found the indifference to this aspect of pornography and the refusal to understand pornography and prostitution as issues of poverty staggering. I don't understand it. I can only assume that people have their racism agenda over here, and their anticensorship agenda over here, and don't bother to see how they are interconnected. But if we do not deal with pornography, we cannot deal with racism in this country. We just cannot.

We need to just keep working at it. When we have pornography in which Black women's skin is being sexualized as something that should be hurt or violated, we are dealing with racism. When women defend pornography, aren't they defending racism, because that's part of pornography? Or pornography in which black men are always shown as rapists—when they defend that aren't they defending racism? Or pornography in which Asian women are lynched, aren't they defending racism when they defend that? I think they are defending racism. But if that is so, then how is it that they continue to denounce racism? What do they mean by it? In my opinion, if we want to fight racism, we need to organize around the issue of pornography as a human rights issue, an equality issue.

woman of power: Is there anything else you would like to say about women in community?

Dworkin: I think we could do better than we're doing. Political movements are not exempt from rules of common decency, common fairness, and common sense. There is no political excuse for reprehensible behavior. I really think that we could do better. I think that we need to pay attention to our ethics, that we really have been exceptionally lax about feminist ethics, and if we don't have an ethical practice as well as a political practice, we can't have a community. That's where I think our attention should be.

Feminist places have to be safe for women. And attacks on women should not be considered acceptable. If we don't spend the time dealing with how we treat each other, we simply can't deal with each other. I can't deal with any of the women who have treated me in these ways until they have apologized.

In terms of what I, myself, can do, I will continue to the best of my ability not to attack individuals, not to retaliate for attacks that have been made on me or other people I love and care about, and I will try to talk honestly about the politics that are involved and the consequences that are involved. But I must say I do think that I've been on the receiving end of it.

I also think that the women who have not spoken up need to speak up. That is important if we are going to talk about women in community, and that can be a beginning. Women have had our share of injury from men and there's no reason that we should be expected to take it from our sisters. It's very hard watching the dominant brutality move its way into the place that once represented resistance to that brutality. This has gone wrong. It has destroyed what was a political home for many of us.

So the question is, "Is there some way of making a difference?" and women have to decide for themselves what that means to them.

Notes

1. See Andrea Dworkin, "Letter from a War Zone," in *Letters from a War Zone* (New York: E. P. Dutton, 1989), p. 313.

2. The text of the Minneapolis hearings has been published in England as *Pornography and Sexual Violence: Evidence of the Links* (London: Everywoman, 1988). Despite many efforts, however, these hearings have not yet been published in the United States.

3. The mayor of Minneapolis vetoed the ordinance both times it was passed there. Media Coalition and ACLU suits challenging the Indianapolis and Bellingham ordinances have resulted in court rulings that pornography does indeed harm women, but this simply proves its power as speech, and therefore the ordinances may not be used.

4. See *Final Report of the Attorney General's Commission on Pornography* (Washington, DC: U.S. Department of Justice, 1986), p. 756.

5. For example, in 1987, *Penthouse* tried to discredit Andrea by charging that she herself writes pornography, a charge that has since been repeated, always unreferenced, in several books and magazines.

11

Defining Our Own Desires

DEBORAH ANNA LUEPNITZ

———•◆•———

Deborah Anna Luepnitz is a psychotherapist in private practice in Philadelphia, Pennsylvania. Her first book, *Child Custody* (published in 1982), was influential in changing child custody laws in several states. Her most recent book, *The Family Interpreted: Psychoanalysis, Feminism, and Family Therapy*, has become required reading in the field of family therapy and in counseling programs throughout the world. Currently, she is clinical associate professor in the Department of Psychiatry at the University of Pennsylvania School of Medicine.

A lifelong activist, Luepnitz is currently involved in the effort to defeat "managed care" proposals in order to make psychotherapy affordable to all. She participated in the United Nations Fourth World Conference on Women in Beijing, China, in 1995, and hopes to develop an international organization devoted to promoting the rights and well-being of single women everywhere. In her spare time, she acts in community theater, sings, and writes short fiction.

———•◆•———

woman of power: You say in your book, The Family Interpreted, *that "even the best therapy cannot bring about radical social change," but you also view therapy as an "innately political process." What perspective do you think feminist psychology can offer on the subject of women and community?*

Deborah Anna Luepnitz: I think that every political group that I have ever been in—feminist groups as well as other groups dedicated to social justice—has suffered from a lack of self-consciousness about both personal and group dynamics. People who have been in therapy have the advantage of knowing something about the problems they bring to a group; they usually have some understanding of the role that they played in their family of origin, for example.

That knowledge helps us to not simply reproduce that role in organizations to which we belong. The family is, after all, the first community we know, and it imprints itself on us. In that original community, certain behavior was expected or required of us, and other behavior was off limits. We can free ourselves of those expectations only with a lot of effort and struggle. I don't think that people who devote themselves only to causes and who don't also take themselves on as a project can ever free themselves of that original set of limitations.

As women, many of us played a "parental" role as children in the family of origin. In the contemporary family, fathers are absent, either physically or emotionally (the latter of which is probably even more difficult than the former), and so mothers often look to daughters as the other spouse or the other adult. Consequently, a lot of us are vulnerable to the problem of feeling that in any group we join, we have to take charge. We feel we have to serve everyone's needs. The leader who "overfunctions" in this way not only burns out herself but also keeps the other members from functioning up to their capacities.

woman of power: Can you be more specific about the way that attempts to build political associations are affected by psychological and group dynamics?

Luepnitz: The first example that comes to mind is from the anti–Vietnam war movement. I was an undergraduate at Kent State University, which was a very radical campus at the time. We students met constantly in those days to plan demonstrations, or sit-ins, or boycotts. As much as we thought of ourselves as revolutionaries, it was nonetheless true that the men did most of the talking, the decision making, and the shouting; the women were quieter, tried to resolve conflicts, and cleaned up after the meeting. The conscious purpose of the group was to challenge everything our government was doing. The unconscious agenda was to keep everything the way it was—to reproduce our parents' 1950s relationships!

Gender, of course, was not the only problematic issue. I'm sure you have had experiences similar to mine: every antiwar, feminist, or peace-movement group is to some extent undermined by individuals who seem to be there less to plan effective strategies than to flex their muscles, display their gifts, settle a score with their fathers, compulsively break up consensus, or acquiesce to the group's will as a means of not having to think for themselves. Of course, we all do all of these things some of the time, but I'm referring here to people who get locked into a rigid position in a group—perhaps a position that they played for very good reasons in their family of origin.

I will give two examples. If a woman grew up in a family where expressing her desires or daring to disagree was treated as treason, which is true in many alcoholic families, she may become the yea-sayer in the group. Let's say she finds herself in a group where she sees better than anyone else something in the group process that is racist or homophobic. She says nothing, because confrontation is so difficult for her; instead she leaves the group.

On the other hand, if a girl grew up in a family full of depressed adults, she may have been stuck with the role of the "bad girl"—the sassy, outspoken one, whose antics seemed necessary to enliven the inexpressive, never-spontaneous parents. Not having had a chance to reflect on these dynamics, however, she goes into women's studies meetings and is always petulant, contrary, and unhappy unless she is creating a scene about every opinion she has.

What I am saying here is really quite simple: the unanalyzed personal can prevent the political.

woman of power: How do you think that women can make bridges between personal and political work?

Luepnitz: The question is often posed, "Shouldn't we mobilize women who have been abused in some political way? Shouldn't the victims of incest be in consciousness-raising groups rather than in therapy?" and "Isn't the ultimate empowering experience for women to construct some kind of social change and not just look inward?"

If the issue is posed in that binary way, we are in trouble, because both are important. Women who try to just "put the past behind" them, and who just forge ahead in order to serve others, will always bring their pain along with them. If you try to change society out of a sense of your own powerfulness and self-love, it means something totally different than if you are really trying to change your own family and are filled with self-hatred. You are capable of a very different kind of political act.

I like the maxim, "Change the world; start with yourself." I think that self-critique is a precondition of collective action; it is preparatory to community. It wouldn't be a bad thing if women could choose as part of their developmental scheme to undertake the personal journey called psychotherapy or psychoanalysis, then experience group therapy, and then move outward to politics. When they have completed therapy, many of my patients express a desire to become more active in the public sphere.

woman of power: Perhaps you could tell us more about the family therapy you do. How do you define "family"? Is family therapy compatible with feminism?

Luepnitz: I like to use Letty Cottin Pogrebin's definition that a family consists of at least one child and one adult who live together and who make emotional claims on each other. It's a good definition because it clearly can include parents who are biological, adoptive, single, married, straight, or gay.

Family therapy and feminism have been seen as contradictory by those who have watched the master family therapists blame and insult mothers and elevate fathers. Their idea is that the mother can take the heat and that the peripheral father needs to be gently cajoled into doing his job. I consider this behavior egregious—the father-coddling is just as disrespectful to the men as the mother-bashing is to the women. I was so disturbed by what was going on in family therapy that I quit my job to write a book about it. Other feminists reached similar conclusions—some before and some after me. We have tried to develop other ways of practicing, of actually using family therapy to empower women.

woman of power: Can you describe the goals of feminist family therapy?

Luepnitz: I believe that every therapist works with a certain *telos*—a sense of purpose about her work—whether it is conscious or not. The *telos* of some therapists is simply symptom relief—or "relief-plus-insight." My *telos* is based on what I see as the fundamental problems of the contemporary family: it is patriarchal, father-absent, and isolated from the community. When a family comes to me because a child is failing school, or setting fires, or not eating, I try to help the family solve this problem, but not just in any way—in a way that will also leave them less patriarchal, less father-absent, and more connected to the community than before.

In addition to families, I also see a lot of single women in therapy. What brings most of them in is loneliness, the cure for which, they are sure, is a relationship. Mainstream therapists unthinkingly subscribe to the message our culture gives us, i.e., "Happiness is a heterosexual romance." Feminist therapists, I think, are more sophisticated. We don't think there is only one kind of happiness for women. Some of those women would be happier with another woman. But much of the longing for romance is a disguised desire for the sustaining power of community. What psychotherapy does is to help women to question familial and cultural assumptions and to define their own desires.

woman of power: What is your opinion of the filtering down of psychological concepts into the popular culture?

Luepnitz: People talk derisively about this being a "therapeutic culture," but I don't share the derision. Every culture has its healers and healing practices. Western culture may be unique in attaching shame to these practices, instead of honor and dignity.

People have to be able to tell their own stories. When someone tells me that she has already been in a twelve-step program or read some popular psychoanalysis, I consider it a head-start. In psychotherapy, you may want to do all kinds of things with those concepts: challenge them, deepen them, and evaluate them in any number of ways, but I think it is good that these ideas are filtering down.

One of the criticisms of therapeutic culture is that people sometimes identify themselves as victims of early trauma and make that their entire self description. But I prefer this culture to the one in which women had no words for the sexual and other abuse they were experiencing. I spent seven years getting a Ph.D. in clinical psychology, and no one ever used the phrase "sexual abuse."

woman of power: You include a section in The Family Interpreted *on the positive contributions made by the African American family, especially with respect to a sense of community and kinship. How can this and other racial/ethnic contributions be incorporated to create a more multicultural psychoanalytic theory and practice?*

Luepnitz: In *The Family Interpreted,* I wrote the first psychoanalytic history of a Black family because mainstream sociologists have depicted African

American families as pathological, and I wanted to point out what is strong and exemplary about them, as well as some of the problems they have.

In some African American families, the structuring of child care approaches what some observers would consider ideal: children are loved and nurtured by more than one adult, and children of both sexes are expected to be involved in helping mothers with children. Moreover, because Black women tend to come from generations of mothers who have worked outside the home, they are more able than their white counterparts to pass on a belief in women's assertiveness and strength, and this is certainly an important aspect of building a healthy community.

woman of power: Also in The Family Interpreted, *you describe the therapeutic situation as providing a "holding or facilitating environment," where childhood wounds can be healed. Do you think that women sometimes expect to find just such a "holding environment" or "safe space" in the women's community, and then experience disappointment or betrayal when that expectation is not met?*

Luepnitz: Yes, I think so. A lot of women turn to women's community in search of "the good mother." Having been silenced and used in the workplace, in families, and in male-dominated public life, they turn to the feminist community expecting a perfect haven. The results can be bitterly disappointing. The most interesting question to me is, why? Why do both women and men expect so much more of women as individuals, and of women's groups? I think that psychoanalytic theories provide the best answers. Dorothy Dinnerstein, the feminist psychologist, wrote a lucid account of some complex psychoanalytic ideas in *The Mermaid and the Minotaur: Sexual Arrangements and Human Malaise.* In that book, she asks why every culture splits the image of woman into good and bad—giving and self-sufficient versus insatiable and withholding. She points out that even after we have realized that society has deliberately shaped these images for us, it is nonetheless difficult to change our expectations. Dinnerstein says that this universal ambivalence towards women has to do with the fact that for every human being, woman is the first "other" and is the container of our most primitive rage and pain. Woman is our first witness and first boss. It is she whom we associate with our desperate longings for nurturance and with our fears of being abandoned.

In infancy, we are not immediately aware that mother is actually separate from our self rather than being an appendage of us. Throughout life, it seems, we continue to have difficulty seeing mothers as subjects with their own needs. By the time we contact our fathers, if we ever do, we are more developed creatures; we have more speech, locomotion, and autonomy. There is always a tendency to be able to forgive fathers—to see them as fallible creatures, bounded by their circumstances. We don't as easily forgive our mothers. To us, as infants, mother was either "good" or "bad"—gratifying our needs, or failing to gratify them. As adults, perhaps the more we feel ravaged by the slings and arrows of the world, the more we long to return to the good mother—real or imagined—of earliest childhood. Incidentally, Dinnerstein thought this primitive thinking about women would only change when men, too, begin to take on the burdens of childcare from infancy onward—when men, too, are the objects of humanity's primordial projections.

woman of power: How does this "good mother/bad mother" dichotomy affect political movements?

Luepnitz: The backlash against feminism is full of examples of this longing for the perfect mother. One example is in Sylvia Hewlett's book, *A Lesser Life,* where she states that she started out "in awe" of the women's movement but that in trying to "do it all"—i.e., have children and a career—she discovered that we still have too little day care, that most men are still not doing any housework, and that we have continued discrimination in the workplace.

Whom does she blame for all of this? The women's movement! How could such an intelligent women miss the transparent fallacy of her argument, given that the movement has been the main source of advocacy on these issues? Women like Sylvia Hewlett initially personify the women's movement as the good mother, and, when they find it lacking, flip their personification of the movement to the bad mother—the source of our troubles, something to reject and attack.

Secondly, I would say that even women who identify with the women's movement have a tendency to mistreat our female leaders—to expect them to be flawless, selfless, and heroic. It's unfair but not difficult to understand. Many of us are doing things our mothers never dreamed of and could not tell us how to do. We are filled with longing for that kind of counsel, for older women who will teach us what we ourselves are now being asked to teach younger women. The idealization and devaluation of women's community and of individual leaders is in part a reflection of our current condition as women who are trying to invent ourselves.

In psychoanalytic theory, it is considered an important developmental achievement when the child learns that the mother is a complex being—that the mother who feeds and rescues is the same one who disappoints and fails. We need to realize that the same movement, the same leaders who let us down on some issues, have also, in innumerable ways, saved our lives as women. If we can go a little easier on "them," we'll be able to go a little easier on ourselves as well.

woman of power: How do we set goals for what can be accomplished in a political setting as opposed to a therapeutic setting?

Luepnitz: I would say that the trick is to bring the wisdom of each into the other without turning political groups into therapy groups or vice versa. When I was working at a women's studies college in Buffalo, after each meeting we had fifteen minutes for criticism/self-criticism. It was very helpful, because it concretely lent recognition to the fact that personal issues sometimes confound political issues. So, for example, during "crit/self-crit," you could say, "I felt a lot of pressure in this meeting to form a quick consensus, and my suggestions weren't heard." And then the group responded: "Actually, you were not as clear as you needed to be," or "You're right." In this way, small annoyances were less likely to grow into rifts and mutinies. Maybe we need to rediscover some of those techniques that were a staple of 1970s feminism.

I am always looking for ways to make links between women and between our personal and our political lives. Family therapy can be very empowering to women. It doesn't have to simply reproduce the power relations of the external society. I have helped a lot of women in family therapy to find their own voice, and to move out of the private sphere for the first time.

woman of power: You speak of the importance of understanding the history of the family. Is it also important for women to understand the history of our own political movements? How can we do this?

Luepnitz: It is crucial. I heard Betty Friedan say in a speech at a NOW convention that many young women have the attitude, "I'm not a feminist, but I want to be an astronaut." She added that young women *should* feel that such choices are their birthright but that we are all diminished if we don't know how it has been for our mothers and grandmothers who could never have done such things. My own grandmother had twelve children and couldn't even write her own name. This has made the ability to write and to lead a different kind of life very precious to me. In that speech, Friedan also said, "How can you say you're not a feminist if you've never worn a girdle?" It is the daily, bodily experiences of a people that create the impetus for social change.

Part of my own sense of community comes from volunteering in the NOW office when I can. There is no education like listening to seventy-year-old and twenty-year-old feminists talk about their lives as they address envelopes together. What will move more women of all ages to start talking and organizing and volunteering again? One answer is clear. By the time this magazine goes to print, *Roe v. Wade* may have been overturned or eviscerated. It is a national scandal and a huge heartbreak. There cannot be any healthy families unless there is motherhood by choice. Certainly, this and other issues will stir a lot of people to political action again. That's the only bright side of this.[1]

woman of power: To talk more personally for a moment, how did you first come to experience community? What constitutes community for you now?

Luepnitz: At present, my community consists of a group of close women and men friends, my students, my amateur theatre group, and a network of beloved feminists I've met in my travels, from Seattle to London to Auckland, New Zealand. My experience of women in community started in high school—in a Catholic girls' school. It was a very loving and fostering place. Intellectual life was rich and abundant, and the world was run by women—powerful and dedicated women who were spirited and fun and brilliant. There were no boys around to compete with, no "math anxiety," and no competition for clothes since we wore uniforms. It was a sort of tiny feminist socialist society where class differences were obscured. That's where I got hooked on sisterhood. I can't help but wish every woman could experience that some time in her life—the experience of living in a community of women.

Notes

1. As far as the history of the women's movement goes, there is one common misunderstanding that I try to correct wherever possible, and it has to do with reproductive choice. Most people will tell you, "Abortion became legal for the first time with Roe *v.* Wade in 1973." The truth is that abortion was legal from the colonial period until the late 19th century, when individual states began to criminalize it under pressure from the Catholic Church. Abortion became legal *again* in 1973.

Why is this fact important? First of all, the Supreme Court judges mentioned it when formulating the *Roe* opinion, and we women should know at least as much about this issue as the men making the laws. More importantly, facts like these remind us that progress is not guaranteed. Justice does not evolve on its own just because the world becomes older. Rights are won only with the sedulous efforts of people working together, and yes, those rights can be lost!

12

Everyday Women's Values

KAREN BRODKIN SACKS

Karen Brodkin Sacks teaches anthropology and women's studies at the University of California at Los Angeles, where she has directed the Women's Studies Program. A longtime activist and feminist, she is a member of Common Threads, a Los Angeles–based group supporting garment worker unionization.

Sacks writes about and researches the issue of women and social change. She is author of numerous articles and books, including *Caring by the Hour,* a study of hospital worker organizing in North Carolina; *Sisters and Wives,* on women in African history; and *My Troubles Are Going to Have Trouble with Me* (coedited with Dorothy Remy), a collection of case studies on women and work. *Race, Class, Gender and the Jewish Question* is her most recent book.

woman of power: *As a cultural anthropologist who is also an activist, your work is closely related to the theme of "Women in Community."*

Karen Brodkin Sacks: My research is focused on working-class women, everyday women, and how women make community, especially in the process of social movements. I focus on these women and their issues because I think that that is where change comes from and that women are really in the center of social movements in terms of contributions and leadership. I'd like that publicly recognized so that women can acknowledge their strengths and skills.

I was involved in community, antiwar and college teacher union organizing in the late 1960s and 1970s. Even though the women's movement was growing by leaps and bounds, there was a stereotype on the Left, and even among some feminists, that working-class women were conservative, family-centered, and had narrow horizons. As a result, working-class women weren't taken seriously by most movements at the time. My first lessons in politics and feminism had come in the early 1960s from African-American women in Boston CORE. They ran the organization, set its priorities, and got things done. Their family responsibilities didn't make them conservative. I found that women were like that in most groups I worked in, so I wanted to break down some of the stereotypes about working-class women, to make their issues and their contributions visible and part of the political agenda. That's why I began the research I did.

In this connection, I wrote a book called *Caring by the Hour,* which is about the kinds of workplace culture and communities that women hospital workers created in the process of trying to unionize at Duke University Medical Center in Durham, North Carolina. Eighty percent of the hospital workers were women; they were nurse's aides, clerks, and so on. The women who were at the center of that drive, the practical leadership, were Black women—although white women and men were also involved. I was dealing with the kinds of skills and strengths that women had in coordinating and giving medical care.

These people were in entry-level positions that were vital to the functioning of the hospital. Of course, the hospital did not recognize that fact and wasn't prepared to pay its workers what they were really worth. So it was important to bring out those kinds of skills and to show that they were based on women's workplace communities where they shared values and recognized each other's strengths and on the basis of that were able to come together and demand respect and acknowledgment of what they were doing. I was pleased to hear that one of the hospital unions in Philadelphia has used whole chunks of *Caring by the Hour* as part of a union-organizing manual. I felt really good about that.

woman of power: Why do you think those women were able to work together instead of competing or coming into conflict with one another?

Sacks: Well, I think conflict is a part of community; people conflict with one another as well as cooperate with one another. I don't want to paint an unrealistic picture of that situation; the union drive ultimately did not succeed, but it came close. The union drive at Duke University Medical Center, which grew out of the civil rights movement, lasted for more than fifteen years. So it had a tremendous wellspring of strength in the Black community in Durham and they were able to reach out to white workers with some success. White workers were able to see that there was a lot to be gained from joining with Black workers.

Another thing that made this drive so successful was that there was interdependence. It was very clear that people who worked with each other needed to rely on each other to get their jobs done. So they were able to see and respect each others' skills. It was also very obvious that the hospital administration was disrespecting them and treating their jobs as if they required no more than clerical skills when in fact they were administrative jobs. And this scenario is, by the way, not unique to that hospital. This is characteristic of hospital work throughout the country.

woman of power: What allows for that shared sense of struggle—the degree of adversity?

Sacks: If you are to bring about change, you have to be in a situation where you can rely on other people, and adversity certainly makes you do that. But adversity is something most folks in the United States are facing today, so although those are necessary conditions, they are not sufficient conditions. One of the big mysteries of life is why, in political work, people rise up angry when they do, and why sometimes people do not rise up when they are just as angry. In organizing work, nobody can ever quite predict the moment. I think that at some level most people in the United States are living under varying degrees of adversity today, so the reasons to come together are certainly there.

The other thing that I think is important to recognize is that, particularly in workplace communities, in everyday jobs where women are concentrated, such as clerical jobs and service occupations, women develop a kind of counterculture, which involves shared values that are counter to the values expressed by their bosses or even their customers. For example, the whole wage system in the dominant ideology says that your value as a human being is measured by your worth in wages, so if you are in a low-wage entry-level job, a clerical job, you are not worth very much. But you live that job, and you and your coworkers know how difficult it is. Women are commenting on that disparity all the time and acting to validate each other. That is a common basis for acting together to challenge things.

In order to be willing to come together, people also need a sense of hope. I am afraid hope is a little hard to come by these days. The future looks so bleak. We tend to think people are apathetic but I don't think that is the case. I think apathy is a surface manifestation of lack of hope. So I think that if we are concerned to challenge the status quo and to put more democratic values into practice, the kinds of values that people have to live by in terms of their interpersonal relations, there has got to be some indication that you can fight city hall and that you can still trust your neighbors.

woman of power: How would you like to see women build community within the feminist movement in the 1990s?

Sacks: I think we have to start from the actual types of communities that women already have, and not think that we need a single women's community. That is certainly not going to happen.

I would like to see us give more attention in the feminist media to the difference between the feminist agenda and the agendas of working-class women and women of color who don't necessarily define their work as feminist. For example, there are many groups of women across the United States and Canada who are trying to halt the dumping of toxic waste and the degradation of their community's environment, or the groups of low-income tenants who are trying to buy or manage their housing complexes. There are hundreds of groups like the Love Canal group and lots of protests led by working-class women and women of color against toxic-waste dumping. That is not surprising since most of the dumps are in poor communities, especially African American and Latina communities.

In Los Angeles, the Mothers of East Los Angeles are working-class Mexican-American women who have been very successful in preventing the state of California from putting a toxic-waste incinerator right on their doorstep.[1] There is also a tenants group in one of Los Angeles's largest apartment complexes, the Lincoln Place Tenants Association, which is organizing to stop the owner from tearing it down and building luxury condos. Low-income and elderly citizens are spearheading a promising effort to turn the complex into nonprofit, mixed-income rental housing. Groups like these practice democratic values because their only power comes from expressing the will of their members.

You have to do something positive and different if you want people to keep coming back and participating. If they don't participate, the group has no influence. Groups like these are places to look for alternative, democratic kinds of values, alternatives to the way social life is organized today. Whenever an organization forms to create progressive change, embedded in that organization is a vision for just and humane social relations.

One of the things I would like to see is a dialogue on visions and values between women from these local groups and, for example, ecofeminists who have been thinking very differently about the environment and the future. There is some common ground there, so I would like to see some coalition building across the lines of class and race and sexual orientation. But in order to do that, it is important to recognize that people have different experiences and perspectives. Oftentimes, when people come together across those lines, there is a tremendous amount of defensiveness and fear of conflict and the discussion stops before it even starts.

To build community in the 1990s, I think we have to really home in on the conflicts instead of glossing over them. But we also need to approach them with an eye to first finding out where the common ground is and then be willing to acknowledge not only that we have different perspectives but also to follow through the implications of each way of looking at things. We also need to be willing to recognize that one set of perspectives may be more helpful than another if we are to solve everybody's problems. I think that some serious working through of conflicts is going to be needed, and we tend to duck conflicts. For example, whites may say, "Oh, I don't see race in this situation." They try to wish the problem of racism away. But it doesn't go away by ignoring it.

woman of power: Do you have any ideas about how we can develop trust across these lines, especially with respect to privilege?

Sacks: There are some fairly clear things to do, although I won't say they are simple. If we are white we have race privilege, if we are middle class we have class privilege, if we are heterosexual we have heterosexual privilege—we need to look really clearly at what those privileges are and acknowledge them.

Yet acknowledging our privileges does not mean feeling guilty about them. Guilt is immobilizing and stems from not being willing to acknowledge those interests and privileges. In any kind of dialogue, you have to be willing to recognize that both parties have interests. For example, as a white woman I have interests and privileges that I have to be willing to address, to say "Do I have to give this up and am I willing to give this up to form a coalition or an alliance?" It is important to recognize that we can be privileged in some ways and oppressed in others.

woman of power: Do you think that women can better address obstacles to community by reconceptualizing conflict as an opportunity to exchange information?

Sacks: Yes, and to problem solve, to stand in one another's shoes and to see ourselves as others see us and gain some insights that way. I see much greater attention to issues of race and class and sexual orientation in the white women's movement, but we have a way to go.

I think that the emphasis on a multicultural curriculum and actions taken towards that objective are just wonderful. They are not confined to women's studies but are going across the whole curriculum and I think that is exactly what we need more of. The issue of multiple perspectives is a really important one because white and middle-class feminism has had a tendency to think of itself as speaking for all women. So I think that developing greater self-consciousness is very important on the part of women who are of the dominant class and color.

The other place I think one learns is in trying to build practical coalitions. Communities and coalitions have a lot in common. Communities are intense kinds of coalitions that cooperate around particular commonalities. Both of them take a certain kind of courage and faith. We are seeing more and more coalitions formed around particular issues such as reproductive rights and toxic waste.

woman of power: How can we learn to regard conflict as a challenge rather than a problem?

Sacks: I don't really have any great insights except to say that when people come together around a common interest, they do in fact learn to do that. When you have to cooperate, then you begin to think more creatively about ways of doing it.

Sociologists Reeve Vanneman and Lynn Weber Cannon analyzed racial conflict in working-class movements and found that it was usually the consequence of failure rather than its cause.[2] They found that when there was a common issue, people were able to overcome racial barriers but that dissension came in only after the movement fell apart. In most movements I have been in, people tear each other up when they have lost the battle, so it is important to maintain hope.

There is another issue that I would like to bring up and that is the kinds of values that are imbedded in working-class women's lives. We have to know what we are fighting for as well as what we are fighting against. I mean that in the practical sense of values and ways of relating to one another. By now, we have a tremendous amount of feminist scholarship about women of all races in factory, clerical, and service workplaces and in working-class neighborhood organizations and the kinds of counter-cultures they have built in everything from union drives to tenant and environmental organizing.

What keeps these groups together is shared goals, cooperation, mutual respect, and trust among their members. Their dislike of hierarchy, competition, and self-aggrandizement goes against dominant values, and women's activism goes against the notion of women as nonpolitical and confined to a private sphere. These values have their historical roots in working-class women's daily lives, where women had neither the time nor the money to handle all their responsibilities on their own.

My father used to call it "taking in each other's washing." Women learned to cooperate with one another by babysitting, driving one another to the store, doing the laundry, cooking, sharing meals, taking in boarders, and all of these things provided for a very dense network of cooperation.

Women in these networks shared somewhat counter-bourgeois values. An example of this is the one that I gave earlier about how society values you by your salary, but this is not how you value yourself as a working-class woman. In African-American communities, this is not at all the way you are valued; you are instead valued by your service to the community.[3] This was also true in early twentieth-century Jewish and Italian communities,[4] and those values constitute a kind of counter dominant-cultural view.

Anybody who has to live in a subordinate group lives with two languages. You have to speak the boss's English, but your own experiences and socialization tell you that this is not a good language for you. You have a better one for yourself but you have to be bilingual and bicultural. One of the things that feminist media and women's studies programs can do is value this knowledge, demonstrate its importance, and learn from it. We can also show how people across different ethnic groups share similar kinds of values, because there is something very important going on here that is shared.

woman of power: How can we increase respect for one another's differences?

Sacks: It is important to look at this in terms of groups of people and to recognize that something like sexism may not take the same form for a working-class woman that it does for a middle-class woman. Let's say that they are both white. The middle-class woman is, or at least used to be, presumed by the dominant white culture to be delicate and in need of protection, while the working-class woman could be worked to death. The good woman/bad woman dichotomy is a class and race dualism. Both of these ideas are sexist but they take different forms.

If, for example, I talk about sexism from a middle-class perspective and I talk only about the forms that affect me, then I am really missing a lot of the ills of sexism. Take the issue of reproductive rights. For a long time, middle-class women focused on abortion and only abortion, until women of color and working-class women pointed out that reproductive rights included sterilization and funding. It is the same issue, but it has different faces.

I think that what is important is the willingness to recognize where we are socially and to expect not only difference but conflict. We need to learn to work through that conflict in a nondefensive way. That requires us to see ourselves as others see us and to think about that seriously, to hear that and talk about those kinds of things. You can walk a mile in somebody else's shoes and that experience could leave you unaffected. You could say, "Well, that is them and this is me." But the next step is, "How does she see me?" Let's dialogue around that instead of saying, "Oh, no, no, no. You are seeing me all wrong. My way of viewing me is the only way to see me." It gives us a structure to talk about why things look different from where we stand and how we can find ways to solve conflicts.

woman of power: Have your experiences with the Left and other movements provided you with any insight into community building?

Sacks: One of the things I learned from the Duke University hospital workers was about how to take leadership, and I think that is an important idea for the women's movement. The way women made decisions and led was something that was almost invisible and it was quite democratic. Women joined this particular union drive as friendship groups. They created the initial movement out of what were essentially lunchtime conversations. When they finally decided on an action, they already had a community of friends and consequently all of them were willing to participate. They had already established trust and respect among themselves and they knew that they could count on each other. They also had the shared values that they were acting on in a politicized way.

The real but unacknowledged leaders in political work that I have witnessed are what I call "center women" because they are at the center of social networks. You can find them in workplaces everywhere. Center women are extremely attentive to what their friends think and say, and they shape a consensus and articulate it. When they opt out, nothing happens. And when they opt in, there is a mass movement.

The first place that I learned about that kind of leadership was when I started teaching at Oakland University in Michigan. Students and faculty were trying to organize for a childcare center, and we went to the campus "maids" who were Black and white women, mostly in their fifties, and asked them if they were interested in joining us. They said, "Well, our kids are grown, but what we really want is equal pay with male janitors." So we raised that issue also. One day we asked if they would come to an all-university meeting to challenge the president of the university on the issues, and they hemmed and hawed.

At some point, one woman, whom I now know was the "center woman," said, "Okay, now listen, girls, you know that either we are all going to go or none of us will, so what are we going to do?" So another woman said, "Well, I guess I could go," and so the center woman said, "Okay we'll be there," and it worked! They walked into that meeting as a group and the university president turned green. It was a very powerful statement to me about democratic process and solidarity.

The nature of that leadership was that it was based on shared friendship and trust, not haranguing anybody with a great new set of ideas. I learned that the direction of the movement comes not from the top but from the bottom. It is built on what people think and feel in their everyday lives. People enter a movement and act as long as they can do so along with the people that they know and trust. I don't think that you just set out to build community any place that you please. Community is based on some kind of daily life interdependence.

And it is a pretty good bet that if we are not willing to be somehow interdependent, we are not going to have a community.

Notes

1. For more information on toxic waste sites, see United Church of Christ, Commission for Racial Justice study, 1987. To find out about grassroots campaigns against toxics, contact The Citizens Clearinghouse for Hazardous Waste. For more information on Mothers of East L.A., see Mary Pardo, "Mexican-American Women Grassroots Community Activists: Mothers of East Los Angeles," *Frontiers* XI (1990) 1: 1–7.

2. See Reeve Vanneman and Lynn Weber Cannon, *The American Perception of Class* (Philadelphia: Temple University Press, 1987).

3. See especially, Bonnie Thornton Dill, "The Dialectics of Black Womanhood," *Signs* 4 (1979): pp. 543–555.

4. See Elizabeth Ewen, *Immigrant Women in the Land of Dollars* (New York: Monthly Review Press, 1985).

13

Envisioning a
Partnership Future

RIANE EISLER

Riane Eisler is the author of *Sacred Pleasure: Sex, Myth, and the Politics of the Body—New Paths to Power and Love* (HarperSanFrancisco, 1995). Based on seven years of research on the hidden history of sexuality and what it means for our lives today, the book follows her international bestseller *The Chalice and the Blade: Our History, Our Future,* hailed by Princeton anthropologist Ashley Montagu as "the most important book since Darwin's *Origin of Species.*"

Born in Vienna, Eisler spent her childhood in Cuba and later studied sociology, anthropology, and law in the United States. She has taught at the University of California and Immaculate Heart College, and is a member of the General Evolution Research Group and cofounder of the Center for Partnership Studies. She is a dynamic speaker who inspires audiences worldwide.

Eisler is coauthor of *The Partnership Way: New Tools for Living and Learning* with her husband, social psychologist and futurist David Loye. She has contributed to many publications, including the first *World Encyclopedia of Peace, Political Psychology, Human Rights Quarterly, Humanities in Society, International Journal of Women's Studies, Futures,* and *Behavioral Sci-*

ences. Her earlier books include *Dissolution* and *The Equal Rights Handbook.* Her groundbreaking work has been translated into most major languages, bringing a new perspective to our past, present, and the possibilities of our future. As novelist Isabel Allende said of Eisler's work, it "opens the spirit to unimaginable possibilities . . . that can transform us."

———————•◆•———————

woman of power: What directions would you like to see feminists take in this decade to facilitate leadership?

Riane Eisler: I think we need to reframe the political agenda. The ways in which politics conventionally have been defined have maintained inequitable relations. This is even true of definitions of human rights, which is why I developed a new, integrated "partnership" model for human rights that does not so absurdly split off the rights of the majority— women and children—from "human rights," as merely "women's rights" and "children's rights."

We in the feminist movement have long provided an analysis of politics that includes the so-called private sphere, emphasizing that "the personal is political." We recognize that there is constant interaction between the private and the public spheres, so we have tried to shift the focus of discourse in politics. We have been partly successful in the sense that issues that were once excluded from politics are now included: sexual harassment, wife-battering and murder, child-beating, rape, sexual preference, reproductive choice. But we need an integrated political agenda that points to all the connections between "women's issues" and the central issues of our time—from the population explosion and the threat of nuclear war to the hunger, poverty, brutality, and ecological devastation all around us.

To a large extent, this has been the focus of my work, which identifies patterns or configurations that are not visible using conventional male-centered approaches. Taking into account the status of women made it possible to see that underneath the great variability of human societies are two basic configurations that I have called the partnership and dominator models. My research shows that the more male-dominant a society or period is (be it Nazi Germany, the Samurai period of feudal Japan, or Khomeini's Iran), the more authoritarian and warlike it tends to be. Conversely, where we see more equal partnership between women and men (as in the Scandinavian nations, and Hopi and Pueblo tribal societies), we also tend to see a more equitable and peaceful society. Also, we need to focus on the interlocking systems of gender, race, and class and how these relations are constructed differently in societies that are oriented toward a partnership rather than a dominator model.

We need to focus political discourse on these connections—for example, on how what the leaders of the so-called Christian right preach is not a matter of religion (because there are also partnership teachings in most religions), but of pushing us back to a more rigid dominator model. We also need to show that how the relations between the female and male halves of humanity are structured is of *central* importance, politically, economically, spiritually, sexually, in all aspects of life.

Second, we need to develop more effective ways of communicating. As you know, the leaders of the fundamentalist right are conducting a stealth campaign, in which they are not disclosing their goals. We must continue to disclose our goals, but we must also be judicious about how we do this. When I speak to the general public, I often identify myself as a feminist, but I tend to do it somewhat later in my speech because I don't want my audience to stop listening to me, to close their minds. We need to reach that constituency that shares many of the feminist goals, but is wary of that label because feminism has been so calumnied. I have found that the term "partnership" can serve as an invitation to feminism.

woman of power: How do you propose we implement an integrated feminist agenda?

Eisler: I have written about three interrelated actions. One is an international campaign to end intimate violence and abuse. That is beginning to come together. We need to invite the world's religious and political leaders to join this campaign, and we need to say, "If you are not with us, we know you are against us, and we will expose you as such."

The second action involves education, not only in schools and universities, but through the media. We need to bring attention to the fact that most of what is presented to us as "news," from revolution to murder, places constant emphasis on the power to dominate, to destroy, that is, to inflict pain. This is what I call a basic dominator systems' maintenance mechanism.

As I write in my new book, *Sacred Pleasure: Sex, Myth, and the Politics of the Body* (which reexamines basics such as sex, spirituality, pain, and pleasure from prehistoric to postmodern times), public demonstrations of the power to inflict pain on others have been a mainstay of dominator rule, in both the macrocosm of the public sphere and the microcosm of the private sphere. What, for example, was the crucifixion about? What were the so-called witch burnings about? What are the "honor killings," or stonings to death, of women about? And why do these killings take place in public? These are public demonstrations that the ultimate power in a dominator model of society is the power to inflict pain. Today, public executions in the West have been replaced by the mass media of communication where violence is continually replayed in front of us. I don't think that we have yet grasped just how this cultural environment serves to maintain the dominator system. For example, on television, the victims of violence are disproportionately women and other socially disempowered groups. Men also outnumber women in the images we see on television in a ratio of about two to one. That gives very clear messages about power relations, doesn't it? We know that people learn consuming behavior from TV, what products to buy, so why wouldn't they learn other behaviors, including violence? We have to understand both of these mechanisms: how the media is modeling violence, and beyond that, how it serves the same function as a public display of brutality.

There is much more to be said, of course, about the media, for example, the lack of lead-story news about the very newsworthy things women are doing all around the world—networking and creating new forms of nonviolent activism.

woman of power: And the third goal of an integrated agenda?

Eisler: The third action goal is economic. We still have an economic system that defines itself and defines what is productive in ways that disempower us as women. One of the major ways of changing that system is to find ways of giving economic value to the work that has been stereotypically labeled "women's work." To some extent, over the last two centuries, some value has been given to that work, and some caring work has been monetized—childcare, nursing, social work—professionalizing what was once just volunteer work. That is a very important trend.

Part of the squeeze on the government budget by the Right, which represents an attempt to push us back to an even more rigid dominator system, is to ensure that economic value is not given to the caring work stereotypically considered women's work so that it is not incorporated into the economic system. If they can again make all caring work unpaid volunteer work by cutting funds for social services, women will be back to square one. It is a very dangerous trend.

I have proposed that we truly change our welfare system, not by further devaluing the work of mothering, but by offering women training, support and yes, pay for mothering work, rather than just an allowance for children's shoes or for rent. The current welfare system is just a bureaucratized version of the male-dominated, authoritarian family, where the woman receives an allowance for the children, and her work is not accorded any economic value.

I think we have to get back to "comparable worth," and even beyond this, to a redefinition of what is productive work. Just as we moved away from a mainly agrarian economy in the nineteenth century, we are rapidly moving away today from an economy that is primarily based on manufacturing. We are moving into what is being called a "service economy," and we have seen what that will mean if we do not make basic changes: jobs at McDonald's. First of all, there are not unlimited jobs at McDonald's, and second, that is hardly the way we want to go. Over the next few decades there is going to be a redefinition of productive work as jobs in manufacturing continue to shrink. We've got to get a very early foothold in that discourse.

Before we leave the subject of economics, I want to say something about spirituality. I think that our economic models ignore the very fundamental idea that people need to have meaning in their lives. We need to feel that what we are doing is valuable. This is yet another reason that we need to redesign our economic models so that we reassign value to caring labor, because that is at the core of a meaningful life, isn't it? This takes us back to something that is a central issue in feminist writings: the dimension of relationship with others. This, I think, is a very spiritual dimension.

woman of power: What is your vision of spiritual leadership?

Eisler: There are many different articulations of the feminine vision. But I think that we do have a unifying vision: the vision of a more just, more caring way of structuring all our relations—beginning with the foundational relations between women and men. The task of the leader is to be able to articulate that vision in a way that will inspire other people, and then to elicit from them their highest potential in order to make that vision a reality for others.

For me, that also means working for a society where spirituality is no longer split off from day-to-day activities. I consider the task of healing that split one of the great challenges of leadership: to reintegrate the economics and politics of our daily lives with what we call the spiritual. By "spiritual," I mean a sense of awe, of wonder, and more than anything else, of connection. That is what the partnership model of society is about: "linking" as a primary principle rather than "ranking," so that diversity is valued rather than used to create rankings of domination.

Another aspect of the spiritual is regaining a sense of joy. So, the leader's task, too, is to reclaim for us basic words like "love," "joy," "family," and "values," to reclaim that vocabulary because it belongs to us, not to the dominators.

I think we need to be clear that we don't just mean something esoteric by spirituality. Splitting off the spiritual from our day-to-day lives is integral to dominator politics, working through religious dogmas that tell people that what really matters is not of this world. I am afraid it is something we see also in parts of the New Age movement, this diversion of people from the recognition that there is a need for fundamental social change. We need leaders who understand that you can't talk about spirituality without talking about economics and politics. I think one of our roles as spiritual leaders is to help people to make those connections.

woman of power: So, you would like to see a more integrated definition of spiritual leader?

Eisler: Yes, otherwise all it amounts to is dancing in the woods. Goddess rituals do change our consciousness and help us to bond, but if we stop there, it is like fireworks, which quickly dissipate. The spiritual illumination needs to be applied to real things. If you really want to be a leader, you have to resolve that you want to leave your mark on history, and that is very hard for women to say out loud because of our socialization and circumstances. As I hear myself say it, I think "That's hubris," to use the Greek term. But that is what I want: I want to be part of that process of changing history.

woman of power: It's interesting that you use that word, because "hubris" means challenging the gods.

Eisler: I am challenging the gods! And you are challenging the gods. We have to do just that. We have no other choice. But at the same time that we deconstruct some of the old mythology and expose it for what it communicates, we are also reconstructing it. Part of spiritual leadership then focuses on the process of remything, and we have made a start in that direction.

As I said earlier, I would like to see spirituality become more grounded and integrated; and, most important, connected to social action. The new spirituality is a spirituality of outrage against injustice. To me, the whole notion of an otherworldly spirituality is another way of maintaining misery and injustice right here on earth. We want an embodied as well as a transcendent spirituality.

We do, however, want to salvage the partnership elements of the religious myths we have inherited. For example, the part of the Christian legend about Jesus as a spiritual leader who has the courage to try to make things better for human beings right here on earth. For example, feeding the masses with loaves and fishes, or stopping the brutal killing by stoning of a woman accused of adultery, which was the custom of that time—as it still is in some rigidly male-dominant and authoritarian (or dominator) societies in parts of the world today. We need spiritual leaders who speak about such killings with moral outrage, who have the courage to challenge the men at the top of religious institutions to denounce these practices vigorously or be exposed for their tacit complicity in these crimes against women. In other words, we need leaders who will reclaim the true meaning of spirituality, who will speak of a morality of caring rather than of coercion, a morality characterized by what David Loye in his work calls a "partnership moral sensitivity." I deal with this subject at length in *Sacred Pleasure*, particularly the shameful silence for thousands of "men of God" about sexual and other forms of intimate violence.

woman of power: In The Partnership Way, *you say that you envision a partnership society as being "not devoid of conflict, and not leaderless." Would you elaborate on that idea?*

Eisler: I am so glad that you brought that up because I think that it is one of our major political issues within the movement. We need to stop shooting down our leaders. We *need* our leaders. One of the most destructive things that has happened—not only in the feminist movement, but in most of the countercultural movements as well—is the "rebellion" rather than "reconstruction" problem. Yes, leadership has acquired a bad name because leadership in a dominator society is associated with men whose orders are obeyed out of fear. But rebellion is not the same as the reconstruction of society.

We need leaders in order to move into a partnership society. Here, as in so many other areas, we have to create viable, positive alternatives. Because if all they do is criticize and rebel, countercultures remain peripheral.

woman of power: What kind of leadership do you think we will need in the 21st century?

Eisler: In *The Chalice and the Blade,* I use the symbols of "blade" and "chalice" to represent two different kinds of power. What we are talking about is what in stereotypical terms we might call the "feminization of leadership": the imbuing of leadership with values that in dominator societies have not been considered appropriate values to a "masculine" identity, values such as nonviolence, empathy, and caring. This is not to say that men cannot or do not exhibit these qualities. But in dominator societies, men who do exhibit them are despised for being "effeminate." And this is not to say that all women exhibit these qualities, but these qualities are part of stereotypical feminine, rather than stereotypical masculine socialization. This is still another reason that the mass entry of women into leadership positions is of such great importance.

We need leaders who recognize that the problem is not modern technology but the kinds of technologies that are developed and marketed and how their use relates to a society guided by the stereotypical "masculine" values of conquest and domination, or by so-called "feminine" values like nonviolence and empathy. We need leaders who see that this is not a question of women's or men's biology but of a social and ideological organization that is either a dominator or partnership organization.

As I said, we need leadership that will reclaim moral authority for women, because women have been barred not only from what is conventionally classified as politics, but also from the priesthood, even in Eastern religions where we still find female divinities. This is an extremely political issue, because it ensures that women can speak of morality, if at all, only from a peripheral position. Those who have been given "moral authority" have often used it to justify women's domination by men as divinely ordained. Much that is still taught in the academy today is a scientific update of the same old dogmas that place men at the center and women on the periphery, if women are dealt with at all. And the papacy is, of course, one of the last bastions of total and absolute male dominance.

In this connection, we need leadership to incorporate the history of women's emancipation—our struggle, our humanity, and our contributions—into what is taught in the schools as knowledge and truth. One of the lessons of history is that we will again be put on a forgotten shelf if we do not manage to change the curriculum—from grammar school through graduate school. Women's studies departments have made an enormous contribution, but again, they remain peripheral. We have to get into the mainstream curriculum.

woman of power: Can you say something about the work you are doing in preparation for the 1995 United Nations Fourth World Conference on Women in Beijing, China, in particular on "mainstreaming the rights of women?"

Eisler: Part of the work that we do as leaders is to create new models, new theories. These are not just a matter of academic interest. We *live* by these theories. Look at the historical influence that Freudian and Marxist theories have had. Developing our theories is very important, and then we must mainstream these paradigms, these new views of reality. We must ask: How do we change these institutions? How do we break out of the roles necessary to the maintenance of the old institutional structures? It is always a question of combining vision with action.

At the Center for Partnership Studies, we just completed a study called "Gender Equity and the Quality of Life," an empirical study of eighty-nine countries showing that gender equity bears an enormous relationship to the quality of life, not only for women but for society at large.

woman of power: What can you tell us about the Center for Partnership Studies?

Eisler: The Center is a small, nonprofit organization. We make articles on partnership available to people who request them, and we also disseminate partnership education through conferences. For example, we co-sponsored the "First International Celebration of Partnership" in Crete in 1992, attended by five hundred people from forty countries. Another of our projects was a conference called "Empowering Women," held in Coeur d'Alene, Idaho, in 1993, and attended by nine hundred people. It focused on the integrated model of human rights I have proposed. We helped to raise money for the Partnership Research Group that was founded at the Chinese Academy of Social Science in Beijing. We did the "Gender Equity and the Quality of Life" study I mentioned, and now we are seeking funding for a multimedia art exhibit that the artist Barbara Schaefer is developing on *The Chalice and the Blade.*

So, even though the Center is a very small organization with very little funding, we have established links with other organizations and we serve as a kind of spiritual home for women and men who have been catalyzed into action through *The Chalice and the Blade*—people who recognize that the failure to include the rights of women and children in human rights and other political theories has led to a situation in which there is no foundation for a society that in both the so-called public and private spheres truly respects human rights.

woman of power: Do you have any other ideas about how women can support the leadership of other women?

Eisler: We need to cherish, honor, nurture, and support our leaders, rather than hold them to inhuman standards of perfection. Are we going to snipe at each other, or are we going to say, "I want to remind you that it is important that you be aware." For instance, it is one thing to say "Be inclusive as best you can," and it is quite another to rake a woman over the coals, which is what often happens. That only creates more divisiveness.

One of the great impediments to our success is this unrealistic standard of perfection we demand that women leaders meet, just as we demand that mothers meet it. We need to become conscious that we carry that programming, and I am no exception here. Social movements reflect, and even sometimes magnify, the problems that they are trying to change, and this results in what psychologists call "displaced aggression." You don't dare attack the person who will really hurt you, so what do you do? You attack your own sisters, your own leaders, instead.

Definitions of leadership in the context of the society that we are trying to leave behind and definitions of leadership for the society that we are trying to create are very different. But we still have to function within society as it is, so we have to have standards that are realistic for our leaders and for ourselves.

woman of power: What else would you like to see women do over the next decade to strengthen feminist leadership?

Eisler: First, to stop fighting and to put our house in order, taking into account scientific studies, such as those of the social psychologist Kurt Lewin, that show that in laissez-faire organizations everything eventually breaks down and the authoritarians or dominators rise up again to take over. It is self-defeating to insist that everything must be decided by consensus, except perhaps in situations where small groups of people have been working together for a long time.

I think we need to be very active in a systemic way in every area of society. We need to keep in mind the vision of society that feminists have been imaging for a long time: "We don't want a bigger slice of the existing pie, we want to bake a new pie"—one where human beings are not divided into superior/inferior rankings, beginning with the ranking of the male half of humanity over the female half. We need to show, at every opportunity, that one reason that we need more women in leadership positions is because it is absurd to speak of representative democracy as long as half the population has token representation at best. We need at every turn to make people conscious of the systemic connections I identify in both *The Chalice and the Blade* and *Sacred Pleasure*—that the male as in-group and the female as out-group or "other," and even beyond this, the use of violence by men to resolve conflicts, is a basic model (one that children internalize very early) for precisely the kind of tragedies and crises we see all around us in our world.

I think part of the task of leadership for the next millennium will be to help other women to understand these things and to form alliances with men who understand that you can't simply tack a just and harmonious society onto a fundamentally unbalanced model of the human species. In other words, "women's issues" have to be placed at the very center of the political agenda.

As I describe in the cultural transformation theory articulated in my writings, I look at social systems as dynamic and capable of fundamental change during times of disequilibrium. With respect to women's leadership, we are now in a time of social disequilibrium, and we will continue to be in such a time as we shift from an industrial to what is being called a post-industrial society. As a systems thinker, I would like to see us position ourselves so that we can take advantage of this moment and change the system itself rather than remaining on the periphery.

woman of power: How do you think that can be accomplished?

Eisler: Systems change requires action by many people in many ways. There is no one thing that will do it, but there are certain critical intervention points. We spoke about some of these earlier: the media, the economic system, the educational system. We have to create alternatives. We need to reclaim our history—the history I detail in *The Chalice and the*

Blade. We need to mainstream that history, not only through the inclusion of women's history—and I think women are the classic model for socially disempowered groups—but also through the inclusion of the histories of other socially disempowered groups, and through the issues of racism, poverty, and so on.

Another of the intervention points I mentioned earlier is economics. Would there be such sharp class distinctions if the work that was truly valued was the kind of work that is done in every household: caretaking work? If we could only devise social inventions to give tangible monetary and social rewards for this kind of work—wouldn't that be a great social leveler?

There are many other important intervention points, including something that is already beginning to happen: the reconstruction (rather than only deconstruction) of spirituality. Indeed, our task for the next millennium is the reconstruction of society, and this includes the fashioning of new myths and rituals grounded in our daily experiences that reaffirm the value of the kind of work labeled "women's work" and reaffirm the values stereotypically labeled "feminine."

For example, we have many rites, and properly so, for dying. We have many ritualized ways of hurting other people, such as war and sports, and we have myths idealizing these activities. But because of the devaluation of women and of anything associated with women, we have not had many rites for birthing.

Part of our task is to reconstruct the ritualization of caring—not sentimentally, but in a real way that recognizes that caring touch is the most spiritual of all acts. This is far more spiritual than going off to find union with the divine by yourself on some isolated mountain top. That may be a wonderful thing for grounding and centering ourselves once in awhile. But I think that our yearning for connection with other humans, whether through sexuality or through the erotic in all the dimensions of our lives, is the real basis for the development of what I have called a partnership spirituality, one that is both immanent and transcendent.

woman of power: What is it like to apply these ideas in a global sense? Do you find that women translate them into their own unique, local applications?

Eisler: I hope that women will build on them in their own unique ways. The partnership and dominator models are basic alternatives for social structure and for human culture, transcending all of the differences of geography, and history, and race, and religion. The focus of my work has been Western culture because that is a huge area in and of itself and also it is what I know, where I live, and what I have learned. But there are data indicating that the prehistoric societies oriented primarily to the partnership model I write about in *The Chalice and the Blade* and *Sacred Pleasure* are not unique; such societies existed in all the early centers of civilization, in Asia, in the Americas, and in other places as well.

Through my work, I have been invited to speak at conferences, universities, and even corporations in many parts of the world. I feel very lucky because I am in touch with so many people who are working for cultural transformation. So, in spite of all the bad news, I know that the grassroots movement is strong and growing.

One of the basic tenets of cultural transformation theory is that change does not happen in a unidirectional line. This is a very important thing for a spiritual leader to keep reminding herself and those she is talking with or writing for: that, despite periodic setbacks during the last three hundred years, we have made extremely important changes. In fact, if you look at the long sweep of recorded history, this period—as bad as it is—is one of the best periods in recorded (or dominator) history in which to be a woman. This is still another reason why it is so important to know our entire history, including prehistory, to reexamine it from a gender-holistic perspective.

woman of power: How has your background empowered you to do the work that you do?

Eisler: I think that what empowered me was a combination of many circumstances. I was born in Vienna, Austria, and I had to flee from the Nazis with my parents in 1938, when I was very small. We fled to Cuba where I grew up. So, first of all, I had that experience of being saved by a hair, because we were on the last ship to Cuba before a ship called the St. Louis. That ship was turned back by the Cuban government as part of a Nazi "test case" to see if the world would lift a finger to save the Jews, and it failed to do so. After that, even as a little girl, I felt that I had to do something important with my life.

I also had a role model of enormous courage in my mother. I describe that kind of courage, to stand up against injustice at the risk of your life if need be, as "spiritual courage" in *Sacred Pleasure*. And my mother did just that. It was Crystal Night, the 10th of November, 1938, the night when the streets of Vienna were filled with broken glass from the windows that had been smashed in Jewish homes, synagogues, and businesses. A looting party came to our house and dragged my father off. My mother recognized in the group a man who had worked for the family business, and she became enraged that he should so betray their kindness. She turned to a Gestapo officer and she said, "This is a good man that you have dragged away—I want him back. You have no right to do this." She could have been killed, but she wasn't! They said: Bring so much money to Gestapo headquarters, and we'll give him back to you. So, she saved my father's life and ours as well. If he had been sent to a concentration camp, we too would later have been rounded up and killed, because we would have stayed behind like many women and children did, in the hope that their men would be returned to them eventually.

I think that many years later my mother's example gave me the courage to take intellectual risks, which is what I do. It also gave me the courage to become an activist in the civil rights, women's rights, and ecology movements, and in what I now think of as the partnership movement as well.

When I was growing up, there were no role models of women leaders who were active in the sense that they were shaping culture. There is still no continuity in what is passed on to us historically. Time and time again, we have had to rediscover the tremendously important work of feminists going way back in history. But, when I woke up in the late 1960s, the gradual realization that there was a tradition of women who opposed the injustices of male dominance was of tremendous importance to me. I began to focus on writings such as Elizabeth Cady Stanton's *The Woman's Bible* and her work in the struggle for women's vote. Other women like Margaret Sanger, who did pioneering work on birth control, and Lucy Stone, who did not take her husband's name, were powerful role models for me as well. Reading the biographies of women—that lost heritage of women, some of them even more radical than women today—continues to give me strength.

I hope one day that these biographies—as well as those still to be written about the women who are providing feminist leadership in our own time—will become part of our classics and will be studied in depth like the lives of men who fought for the rights of men are today. But this will not come of itself, this partnership future. It will only come if every single one of us accepts her or his responsibility to take a leadership role in actively working for a more equitable and peaceful world.

Excerpts from *Sacred Pleasure:*
Sex, Myth, and the Politics of the Body—
New Paths to Power and Love

BY RIANE EISLER

Today our sacred images and myths tend to focus more on death, punishment, and pain than on sex, birth, and pleasure. Hence it is not surprising—although once we really look at them, it is shocking—how few of our religious images express love in intimate relations. We have no sacred images of sexual love or sexual pleasure since only sex for procreation was condoned by the Church fathers, and even then only grudgingly. On the contrary, rather than focusing on pleasure, much of Christian religious imagery focuses on pain and cruelty, idealizing and actually sacralizing suffering (as in the endless images of martyred saints and Jesus' martyrdom on the cross). Even our religious imagery of parent-child and sibling relations focuses more on violence (as in the famous story of Cain and Abel) or rote obedience to an all-powerful paternal authority (as in Jesus' obedient sacrificial death).

The old dominator stories and images have a grip on our imagination, particularly on the imagination of our cultural gatekeepers: the academic, religious, economic, and educational establishments, and especially the publishers of books, magazines, and newspapers and the producers of television and radio news, entertainment programs, and films.

So one of the great creative challenges of our time—critical if we are to continue our human adventure in an age when the old ethos of domination and conquest is increasingly dysfunctional, even potentially suicidal—is to create for ourselves and our children images and stories of the sacred more congruent with a partnership than dominator social organization, images and stories in which giving and receiving pleasure and caring, rather than causing or submitting to pain, occupy center stage.

Cultural transformation theory proposes that, in the language of nonlinear dynamics, the dominator and partnership models have for the whole span of our cultural evolution been two basic "attractors" for social and ideological organization. Drawing from chaos theory and other contemporary scientific theories that show how living systems can undergo transformative change in a relatively short time during states of extreme disequilibrium, cultural transformation theory shows how these same principles apply to social systems. Specifically, it shows that many beliefs and practices we today recognize as dysfunctional and antihuman stem from a period of great disequilibrium in our prehistory when there was a fundamental shift from partnership to dominator model ascendency. And it proposes that in our chaotic time of escalating disequilibrium we have the possibility of another fundamental cultural shift: this time in a partnership rather than dominator direction.

This book shows that the degree to which a society orients to a dominator rather than a partnership model profoundly affects the degree to which it relies on pain rather than pleasure for its maintenance. It examines how through a variety of means, including the sacralization of pain rather than pleasure, dominator systems have idealized the institutionalization of pain.

An interesting feature of many of the organizations today springing up as potential nucleations for an international partnership movement is that they have a strong spiritual component. But it is not the old-style spirituality of either detachment from all that is of this world or of charitable endeavors that, while important, focus only on ameliorating the pain of poverty and illness.

It is rather a spirituality that recognizes the responsibility of every one of us to do what we can to eradicate what has been called structural violence: not only the institutionalized use of physical violence, but also oppressive, exploitive, and discriminatory structures that deny people the food, shelter, health care, and education they need to maintain their bodies and develop their minds, or threaten to do so if they organize to change existing values and institutions.

In short, it is a spirituality that puts into actual practice the partnership teachings that lie at the core of most world religions: the teachings of compassion, nonviolence, and caring. Even beyond this, it is a spirituality dedicated to empowering people so they can take action against oppression, exploitation, and discrimination, rather than passively accepting injustice in the hope of a better hereafter in which those who are unjust will be punished and those who patiently accept injustice will be rewarded. Because it is a spirituality that does not consider what is of this world secondary, this new spirituality of empowerment also recognizes that politics can no longer ignore matters that directly impact the human body.

So the relearning of love in all of its forms, beginning with how we can be more loving parents to our children, is not, as conventional wisdom might have it, just a nice little frill to add to our educational curriculum if and when there is leftover funding from basic curriculum needs. If we are serious about creating a more democratic, less violent, truly civilized society, it is a basic curriculum need. It is certainly essential, after so many centuries of dominator socialization, to any realistic hope of freeing our body cells, nerves, and tissues to fully experience and express our powerful human yearning for connection.

If we succeed in completing the shift from a dominator to a partnership world, both the realities and the myths of our future will be very different from what they are now. In this world there will still be myths sacralizing suffering, as pain and death are part of the cycles of nature and of life. But there will be many more myths about the joy, awe, wonder, and ecstasy of physical love.

There will be stories about how we humans are conceived in delight and rapture, not in sin. There will be images spiritualizing the erotic, rather than eroticizing violence and domination. And rather than myths about our salvation through violence and pain, there will be myths about our salvation through caring and pleasure.

THE DOMINATOR AND PARTNERSHIP MODELS COMPARED

Component	Dominator Model	Partnership Model
Violence	A high degree of social violence and abuse is institutionalized, ranging from wife- and child-beating, rape, and warfare to psychological abuse by "superiors" in the family, the work place, and society at large.	Violence and abuse are not structural components of the system, so that both boys and girls can be taught nonviolent conflict resolution. Accordingly, there is a low degree of social violence.
Spirituality	Man and spirituality are ranked over woman and nature, justifying their domination and exploitation. The powers that govern the universe are imaged as punitive entities, be it as a detached father whose orders must be obeyed on pain of terrible punishments, a cruel mother, or demons and monsters who delight in arbitrarily tormenting humans, and hence must be placated.	The spiritual dimension of both woman's and nature's life-giving and sustaining powers is recognized and highly valued, as are these powers in men. Spirituality is linked with empathy and equity, and the divine is imaged through myths and symbols of unconditional love.
Pleasure and Pain	The infliction or threat of pain is integral to systems maintenance. The pleasures of touch in both sexual and parent/child relations are associated with domination	Human relations are held together more by pleasure bonds than by fear of pain. The pleasures of caring behaviors are so-

(continues)

Component	Dominator Model	Partnership Model
	and submission, and thus also with pain, be it in the so-called carnal love of sex or in submission to a "loving" deity. The infliction and/or suffering of pain are sacralized.	cially supported, and pleasure is associated with empathy for others. Caretaking, lovemaking, and other activities that give pleasure are considered sacred.
Power and Love	The highest power is the power to dominate and destroy, symbolized since remote antiquity by the lethal power of the blade. "Love" and "passion" are frequently used to justify violent and abusive actions by those who dominate, as in the killing of women by men when they suspect them of sexual independence, or in "holy wars" said to be waged out of love for a deity that demands obeisance from all.	The highest power is the power to give, nurture, and illuminate life, symbolized since remote antiquity by the holy chalice or grail. Love is recognized as the highest expression of the evolution of life on our planet, as well as the universal unifying power.

Notes

14

Decolonizing Hearts and Minds

MILILANI B. TRASK

Mililani B. Trask is a Native Hawaiian attorney with extensive legal background on Hawaiian land and legal entitlements. She is currently serving a second term as the elected kia'aina (prime minister) of Ka Lahui Hawai'i, the Sovereign Native Nation of Hawai'i, a population of approximately 20,000, and is the chief executive officer of the Hawaiian Nation. Since 1988, Trask has been the executive director of the Gibson Foundation, a nonprofit organization that provides assistance to Native Hawaiians seeking home ownership. She is a founder and board member of the Indigenous Women's Network and in 1993 was appointed by Nobel Laureate Rigoberta Menchu to the Indigenous Initiative for Peace, a global organization of indigenous leaders seeking to advance the rights of indigenous peoples regionally and globally. She served as vice-chair for the General Assembly of the Unrepresented Nations and Peoples Organization at The Hague in 1995 and was awarded a Bannerman Fellowship for activists in 1994. She has worked to organize the Hawaiian community for seventeen years on the issues of sovereignty, self-governance, environmental racism, human rights violations, and land entitlements.

woman of power: As the Native governor of Hawai'i and an activist with considerable experience in the Hawaiian community—and as a member of many global organizations—what can you tell us about your work and how it relates to the theme of this issue, "Leadership: Feminist, Spiritual, and Political."

Mililani B. Trask: My work is primarily political human rights work. It started out that way because, as an attorney, I was interested in resolving historical injustices that had been done to the Hawaiian people by both the state of Hawaii and the United States of America. What I learned when I became involved in political issues is that our perceptions as women very much relate to our cultural, racial, traditional backgrounds. I found that my work, which is primarily political work, became spiritual work as well because the protection of our spiritual practice and sacred sites is a political issue. My work also relates to the health of our communities, women's health, and domestic violence. I consider my political work to be all encompassing because these issues are all interrelated.

woman of power: How has your background empowered you to do the kind of work that you have chosen to do?

Trask: There were several things that pointed me in this direction. The first was my upbringing. My parents were very much committed to educating their children about what it meant to be a Hawaiian in the modern day and age. My parents ensured that all of their children would be raised with a very thorough understanding of what had happened to our people at the hands of missionaries and because of the influence of introduced, Western political ideas. Unlike many other Hawaiians, our family was raised with the understanding that we had once had an independent kingdom, that we had the right to live our cultural lifestyle on our lands, and that these things were taken away by acts of colonialism and imperialism imposed on us by American businesses, and later by the U.S. government and its creation, the state of Hawaii.

Another thing that empowered me to do this work was being raised with a strong religious foundation. We believed very much as a family that there were some things that were right, and that people needed to live in a *pono* way, as we say in Hawaiian, which means "to live with righteousness." We were raised with the challenge from my parents that wherever there was something that was wrong or unjust, we needed to oppose it and to speak out against it.

So, I think that these two influences combined to give me a strong commitment to work in the area of human rights; not only for the Hawaiian people, because my work with Rigoberta Menchu and others has now expanded internationally to include the fundamental human rights of all the indigenous peoples of the world. So, my educational background, my family upbringing, and my strong religious foundation combined to give me this commitment to follow the career that I have chosen.

woman of power: Did you have any female role models for the kind of work you chose?

Trask: Yes. My role models have always been female and they have always been women of color. My greatest role model was my mother, Haunani Trask, who came from a very humble, very rural, traditional Hawaiian background. She was one of eight children, but she was able to get an education, and she committed her life to being a teacher.

She was a role model for me because when times got hard—my father went to prison and there wasn't enough food on the table—she never gave up hope. She used the skills and education that she had to maintain not only herself, as a working mother of six children, but also to continue to educate her children and to provide us with everything that she could.

My second role model was my grandmother on my mother's side, Iwalani Haia. My "tutu" (the Hawaiian name for grandmother) was, in my estimation, the prototypical role model for Hawaiian women. She did not have an education, but she was very well respected in her community where she worked not only with the churches but with the families who were in need. She was a widow with eight young children, and despite her lack of education she raised all of her children to get a good education, to be outstanding citizens. In addition to that, she fed and clothed her family with the fruits of her own labor. She had a small fleet of canoes and she went out in her canoes every day and caught fish. As she got older, others helped her with the canoes so that she could keep food on her table and the tables of many other families in the community.

My grandmother was also available to the community to practice and to teach *Ho'oponopono*, which is the traditional Hawaiian format for conflict resolution. The process of *Ho'oponopono* requires a skilled guide who works with people in conflict to assess the problem from all perspectives and to reconcile opposing positions so that balance can be achieved and negative influences banished. So, my grandmother was a woman with a poor education but a great heart and great integrity, which she passed on to her children and grandchildren.

In the church, in my religious background, I was always able to find female role models who were women of color. Even when I was going to Catholic school as a young girl, the madonna that I always loved the best and prayed to was the Virgin of Guadeloupe. I had a much easier time relating to spiritual figures who were women of color than to other figures, female or male, who were white.

woman of power: How do you think good leadership skills can be encouraged in young women and girls?

Trask: I very much endorse and support the idea of mentoring programs. I think that these programs are essential to passing on leadership skills to younger women because leadership skills are acquired in large part through hands-on experience. Younger women and girls who are striving to become leaders need to have someone who can give them advice when new events arise that they do not have the personal experience to address. In addition, working with an older women who has hands-on experience interjects a personal element into this kind of program; just having someone there as a support person means a great deal. I do not believe that leadership skills can be acquired through academic programs alone. Women need to be out in the field, working closely with other women who have had similar experiences so that they can pass on to the next generation what they have learned through their own lives. I believe this is the only way that we can prevent history from repeating itself.

woman of power: What advice would you offer to someone now embarking on a path similar to your own?

Trask: My advice, especially to women of color, is to hold fast to your culture, your traditions, your background. Remember that what is instilled in you, what is culturally and biologically encoded in you, is the information that you will have to rely upon when you are walking blind and do not have a template to follow. At those times, you are called upon to return to your own personal foundation. And your culture, your background, your tradition, is the *papa*, which means "foundation."

It is important to cultivate and practice a strong religious foundation. I believe that spiritual practice is the wellspring of energy upon which we can rely. Social activism in all its various forms is exhausting; it is often the type of work that is compensated poorly, demands a great deal of time, and puts stresses on personal relationships with family, with children. And many times when you are fighting for human rights, when you are fighting against historic injustices, there are not a lot of people with the integrity, the willingness, or the fortitude to stand with you. When you have a strong religious and spiritual foundation, you will find, in those times of despair, that you are not walking alone.

I want very much to stress that the cultural and traditional backgrounds of women of color provide them with many options for spiritual practice. Many women are Christian and many hold to the traditional practices of indigenous peoples; both can provide sustenance if you really practice with your heart and commit yourself. My advice is to utilize what you have in your cultural background and develop and always maintain your religious and spiritual foundation. You will find that in your work as a leader there will be many times when you are operating primarily because of your faith in yourself and your belief that you can make a difference, and that is a commitment that you cannot get in any other way except through your own cultural background and spiritual foundation.

woman of power: What do you consider the essential facets of effective women's leadership?

Trask: I think that there are many essential characteristics to be addressed. One is the ability to communicate with others through public speaking but also in writing. Leadership skills require that you be able to communicate with clarity in any medium.

Another essential facet of good leadership is the ability to administer and to delegate authority. Leaders have a great deal of power, but if we are to be successful from generation to generation, we need to be able to use our power to empower others.

A third essential facet of good and effective leadership is the ability to resolve conflict. Any leader knows that people will not follow you blindly. If you are a good leader, you want to be able to elicit from people their ideas and evoke a feeling in them that they want to work with you. If you do this successfully with a number of people, you will find that many different opinions will be expressed and that many different personalities will be in the forefront. Some of these personalities may be difficult to work with and there will be many different levels of skill and educational background among them. Conflicts and disagreements can arise whenever you undertake a project, so a good leader has to be able to resolve conflict and have the skills necessary to get people to concede points so that she can create consensus.

woman of power: How have variables such as gender, ethnicity, race, social class, religious background, and/or educational opportunities shaped your ideas about your leadership role?

Trask: All of these variables have had a major impact on the way that I look at my role as a leader and in the way that I continue to perform my role. My educational background (through law school) gave me a very good opportunity to assess different types of information. It also trained me to be an advocate, able to form an opinion, enunciate that opinion, and act as its champion.

I cannot stress enough how gender, ethnicity, and race very much impacted the way that I look at the world and the way that I exercise my leadership role. Women are always called upon to demonstrate more as leaders than men. My background as a woman, as a woman of color, and as an indigenous woman of color has exposed me to a great deal of prejudice, not only because I am a woman, and not only because I am a woman of color, but also because here in Hawaii, as a native Hawaiian woman, I am a member of an indigenous minority that is less well accepted than some other minorities. All of these things, which might be considered detriments by some people, could have been stumbling blocks, but they have given me strengths. They exposed me to racial bias, sexism, and other types of prejudices and taught me a great deal about what it means to be a leader and how leaders must fight for recognition.

woman of power: Have any new questions, theories, ideas, or examples of women's leadership inspired you in the recent past? Also, have any women's movement ideas about leadership influenced your work either positively or negatively?

Trask: I have been inspired greatly in my work both at home in my native Hawaii and in the international arena by the role models that I see emerging globally, particularly among indigenous women leaders. My opportunities to work with women such as Winona LaDuke, Marsha Gómez, and Janet McCloud here in the Native American Indian community; Sharon Ven from Canada; and now, for the past two years, with Rigoberta Menchu, have been a great inspiration for me to continue the work I have undertaken. Rigoberta has convened an assembly of twenty-one global, indigenous leaders to work on the United Nations Agenda for the Decade of Indigenous Peoples and to explore mechanisms for the resolution of political conflict between national states and indigenous peoples.

The Indigenous Initiative for Peace has already been instrumental in stopping bloodshed in Chiapas, Mexico. I believe it is because we have finally come to a point where we are establishing a very strong global network for indigenous women's leadership. Just the fact that we can communicate with each other and rely upon each other, has very much affirmed my commitment to the task I have undertaken.

As far as women's movement ideas about leadership are concerned, I have had both positive and negative responses. In the sixties, I followed the white feminist movement closely; I read all of the appropriate materials, but for some reason it did not strike a chord in me as an indigenous woman. I found that much of the analysis of sexism was applicable to me, but I did not find any decent analysis of racism, ethnicity, and cultural differences. In these very significant areas, the white feminist literature fell far short of what I was looking for.

In recent times, I have been enlightened by the work of my own sister, Haunani-Kay Trask, who wrote a book that I think will be utilized in the future by both white feminists and feminists of color all over the world. *Eros and Power* analyzes from the white feminist perspective some of the issues that have been raised but it also interjects important political, cultural, racial, and ethnic criteria about which white feminists need to be aware. My sister's second book, *From a Native Daughter*, also contains some interesting vignettes on this topic.

If women as a whole are truly going to be able to unify, we have got to be able to overcome our racial, cultural, and socioeconomic differences. I do not believe that there has been any meaningful progress made in this area in the feminist movement and it will not be made until feminists of color and indigenous feminists begin to interject their own perspectives into the feminist arena. I should say that, in general, I consider the term "feminist" to be a term that refers to the body of information and the group of women who are basically white women of privilege.

woman of power: How has your experience of or definition of leadership changed over the course of your lifetime?

Trask: My experience of leadership has changed radically. When I was young, I considered a leader to be someone who got up, spoke, and received a lot of applause, or someone who held public office because many other people had voted her or him into office. So, I defined leadership in this very narrow way.

The experience of my lifetime has led me now to a different definition of leadership. To be sure, leaders in elected political office share certain things in common with other leaders. But a true leader is not often measured in the way that a political leader from the two-party system is measured. My own experience leads me to recognize leadership in many different areas in our communities; for example, many people are leaders because they have developed good health programs or because they are working in very creative ways with our children.

woman of power: What directions would you like to see feminists take in this decade in order to facilitate leadership within local, national, and/or international movements and to prepare women for leadership roles in the next century?

Trask: All women, and especially women of color, need to dedicate themselves to becoming more active in what we consider to be the male-dominated political arenas. In the United Nations, the House and Senate in the U.S. Congress, in state politics, and in the community political arena, the leadership has been primarily male, and the primary focus has always been on male-identified issues.

What we are seeing now, nationally and globally, is a shift as more and more women are entering political office and we are seeing some effects of that. As long as women are relegated to lower levels of political decision-making, we are not going to be able to have a major impact on the national political agenda, including the indigenous nation of Ka Lahui, Hawai'i, the Sovereign Native Nation of Hawai'i, but also the United States and all the nations at the United Nations.

Our community work is important, but developing a strong cadre of feminist leaders—women of color and indigenous women—in these political arenas is critical because we are facing global issues relating to population, development, the utilization of finite resources, and war. Political decisions about these issues are made at very high levels, and we can no longer allow men to dominate these agendas.

woman of power: Are there any changes you would like to see the feminist movement make in order to foster women's leadership?

Trask: The white-dominated feminist movement needs to move over and really engage their indigenous sisters and their women of color sisters in a broader dialog about what feminism really means. We have to realize, for example, that only a minority of women in the world are white and living in the north. If we are going to impact global policy and make regional change, we are going to have to have very strong and clear channels of communication between the feminist leaders of the south, women of color and indigenous women, and their white counterparts in the north. Again, this is a stumbling block that needs to be addressed.

There needs to be some heavy introspection and a political/cultural/racial analysis, as well as a colonial and imperialist analysis of the feminist movement itself so that we can better understand our own feelings of cultural alienation and better understand what racism really means. Once we get over these hurdles, we truly will be strengthening the global feminist movement, and we will really need a united effort if we are going to roll back what is happening in the male-dominated national and international arenas.

woman of power: For what specific issue or issues (such as health care/reproductive rights, the human rights of women, lesbian rights, and so on) would you like to see feminists provide strong leadership in order to prepare us for the next century?

Trask: We have already developed some excellent leadership among feminists on health care and reproductive rights issues. That was demonstrated clearly at the United Nations International Conference on Population and Development in Cairo, Egypt, by the contributions of the U.S. Women of Color Delegation and the participation of the National Latino Health Organization and Native American Women's Health Education Resource Center. In Cairo, it was very disappointing that many women worked with governments to focus the conference on abortion, which was basically the agenda of white women of privilege, rather than on issues relating to dislocated populations and development.

I think that what we need to focus on to prepare ourselves for the next century is feminist, indigenous, and women of color leadership, especially with respect to natural resource management, environmental protection and conservation, and resolution of conflict—there is so much war, and bloodshed, and opposition to creative initiatives; even in our own local communities, there is so much domestic abuse and alcohol- and drug-related violence.

It is critical that women develop leadership with respect to conflict resolution. This includes women in their families and their communities at the local grassroots level, as well as women who work in the area of conflict resolution, nationally and internationally, such as Rigoberta Menchu's work in the Indigenous Initiative for Peace.

woman of power: How can women best support the leadership of courageous activists and visionaries in the feminist, spiritual, and political movements? The leadership of women whose voices need to be heard?

Trask: The first thing to do is to help us get the word out. Women's issues are always being marginalized. Women leaders are always being moved aside. Their issues and their voices can be heard only if we have the assistance of other women to give exposure to what we are saying.

A good example is *woman of power* magazine looking for the voices of women of power and giving them a forum. I think that that is by far the most important support activity that women in leadership roles need. Help us to get the message out; help us get the exposure for the issues and for ourselves as spokeswomen for the issues.

A second way to support leaders is by giving us some actual hands-on support. Women leaders, especially those in impoverished communities, need financing, copy machines, fax machines, paper, pens—the basic tools to get the job done—as well as people with organizing skills and other skills. A lot of people don't have the time to support a struggle, but every little bit helps.

woman of power: What obstacles to women's leadership in the 1990s are of concern to you? How would you like to see those problems addressed?

Trask: The basic obstacles to women's leadership in the 1990s are the same as those we faced in the 1980s: sexism, racism, lack of education among women, impoverished communities, lack of access to public media, and increasingly, also, a lack of good medical care. We need to continue to oppose these obstacles. There is no way to stop racism and sexism except to confront them whenever they appear and to oppose them with everything that we have.

In addition, we need to work with people, both women and men, who are racist and sexist so that they can begin to understand what racism and sexism really mean.

I think that some of the other obstacles are becoming easier to address. For instance, with the media—TV, radio, and press—women in general need to develop better skills so that we better understand what the media is and how to access it. As far as raising funds for media, we need to approach this in the 1990s by accessing technologies like e-mail and Internet, by supporting women's publications such as *Indigenous Women's Network* magazine and *woman of power.*

We also need more women's leadership to challenge the existing media systems. For instance, in the community media, every state now has community network planning, but most of that programming is done by men.

woman of power: What do you envision as the role of women's spiritual leaders during the 1990s and throughout the twenty-first century? How do you think acknowledgment of the sacred empowers women?

Trask: As I touched upon earlier, my own spiritual practice has been the greatest foundation and well-spring that I have. In the 1990s and the twenty-first century, we need to see more women spiritual leaders emerging as community leaders.

Women have the ability and innate sensibility to understand the sacred. I think that women have a much greater capacity to identify with what is sacred, which I think springs from the fact that women can give birth and birth itself is a sacred act. When you understand the ability to make life, you know that it is truly the greatest manifestation of the Creator. It is the Creator who gives us our life and gives life to the birds in the air, the great leviathans of the oceans, the great multiplicity that we call biodiversity. The Creator has this sacred power and women also have this ability to continue the life of their species. Women have the biological ability to understand and appreciate the sacredness of life. This expands beyond our own bodies to the sacredness of the life of the earth, the sacredness of the life of the people and the nations. So the spiritual practice, the spiritual power is really an essential part of what our work is.

woman of power: Is there anything else you would like to say about women's leadership?

Trask: I encourage women to really look within themselves to see what they can do for themselves, their family, their community, their nation, and the earth. I believe that every individual has the ability to acquire leadership skills, but that there are certain individuals who are called upon, who are put on this earth to assume certain responsibilities. It is part of our karma, our cosmic calling.

The only way that you will find your right place in the larger cosmic reality is through introspection. You will need to look inward to consider the skills that the Creator has given to you, to look at all of the obstacles that have been placed in your way, and to realize that overcoming them gives you a great opportunity to acquire the skills you will need to face challenges in the future.

Every human being is on this earth for a purpose, and it is a purpose more important than making money or having people applaud you. By inquiring about and reflecting upon this, let every one of us find her direction and thereafter do all that she can to achieve those things that are brought before her. There is really a personal responsibility in this.

I don't believe that leadership is something that requires recognition. For some of us that is true, but a women can provide leadership in a way that is not going to place her in a position to receive awards, and that does not mean that she is not a leader. So, a personal commitment is an important thing for everyone to internalize and realize.

Indigenous Women, Self-Determination, and Nation Building

A SPEECH BY MILILANI B. TRASK, KIA'AINA, KA LAHUI HAWAI'I

Setting the Agenda

Recently, while attending the twelfth session of the U.N. Working Group in Vienna,[1] I was asked to chair a U.N.P.O. Committee meeting convened to discuss the agenda for the U.N. Fourth World Conference on Women, to be held in Beijing, China, in September, 1995.

As global regional prepcoms proceed, it has become apparent that some of the regional planners have a skewed and limited impression about which of the global issues to be discussed are really "women's issues." This underlying conflict surfaced again in Geneva, Switzerland.

It is commonly assumed that "women's issues" relate to the family, children, nutrition, and health. In recent times, other issues relating to employment, pay equity, and gender bias have been included under the umbrella of "women's issues," due largely to the recognition given to women laborers in the national and global arena.

However, there continues to be great reluctance at local, regional, national, and international levels to accept racism, self-governance, and nation-building as primary issues of concern to women, especially to women of color.

If indigenous peoples, cultures, and nations are to survive, indigenous women need to assert themselves in the ongoing dialogue and debate, and aspire to assume greater authority in the governance of their peoples, nations, and communities.

Indigenous women are literally the mothers of their nations. In this respect, indigenous women are vitally concerned with all of the issues impacting the collective community—the native nation.

In traditional cultures, indigenous women played significant roles in the religious, societal functions of their collective community. The emergence of Western (male-dominated) spirituality that heralded the conquest of the world by European "discoverers" and imperialists had the significant impact of subverting the traditional role of indigenous women in the "political" arena.

Irrespective of the role indigenous women played in their traditional societies, it is accepted as common knowledge that global colonization and conquest destroyed or negatively impacted the vast majority of the world's traditional cultures. The historical tragedy of the past and the assimilationist policies imposed by colonization have cast indigenous women aside or relegated them to subservient, marginal positions in today's world.

This oppression should be viewed as a primary political threat to the survival of indigenous peoples in the modern context. Consequently, its eradication should be a central goal of all indigenous peoples and the paramount objective of indigenous women who are committed to the survival of their cultures, communities, and nations.

Decolonizing Our Minds and Hearts

Self-determination as an international legal concept refers to the right of peoples to freely determine their political status and to freely pursue their economic, social, and cultural development. The exercise of one's self-determination requires that there be true freedom of choice. This implies not only freedom from the external control of other sovereigns, but freedom from the internal controls and psychological obstacles that are the legacy of past colonization.

Indigenous women who are engaged in social, health, economic, and political work amongst their own peoples need to prioritize their own empowerment as the central undertaking of their work. Unless this critical element of self-reflection and self-development is pursued by indigenous women (individually and collectively), we will continue to be ineffective in our undertakings, and we will continue to hold a marginal position in our own native nations and in the broader national and international arenas.

Our Cultural Wellsprings

As indigenous women, we have rich traditions upon which we can rely and from which we can and should draw our sustenance. Primary in all traditional societies were the religious practices that provided the foundations of our cultures and governments. Acknowledging our spiritual belief systems and incorporating them to the greatest extent possible in our daily lives are keys to self-empowerment and self-determination for indigenous peoples. The actual practice of ceremonial worship and cleansing is a fundamental part of our individual and collective identity as indigenous peoples. We need to be bold enough to assert the traditional spiritual practices of our cultures in nontraditional arenas, including our work with tribal governments, the United States government and the United Nations.

All traditional societies recognized the inherent relationship between Mother Earth, human and other life forms, and the Sacred. Only in Western cultures has the secular model been embraced. The separation of peoples from the Creator and the Earth has brought us to the present state of global imbalance, regional warfare, destruction of the environment, poverty, and tragic violations of human rights. If this process of deterioration is to be halted and reversed, secularism as a barrier to personal and political empowerment must be replaced by the holistic approach genetically and culturally encoded in us.

There is no way that we can escape the ultimate realization that we ourselves are the vehicles for change. Achieving this paramount objective in our lives is the greatest accomplishment because from this flows our continued commitment to the struggle for our lands, families, and inalienable human rights. From this wellspring flows our resiliency—as women, as the mothers of our nations, and, collectively, as indigenous nations.

Returning to the Visions of Our Elders

Nation building is everyone's work. The survival of the nation depends upon the collective effort of all facets of a society. In traditional times, before the coming of the "white man," the interrelatedness of all of a society's diverse aspects was acknowledged. Today, as the result of imperialism, colonization, and assimilation, people believe, mistakenly, that they are not really part of the government.

Government and the political arena are viewed by many indigenous women as the province of "elected tribal leaders," or Western politicians with affiliations to national partisan organizations. This belief is widely held by the white majority in most industrialized countries who avoid politics and who refuse to vote or participate in any way in the "political" arena. Generally speaking, most people feel alienated and intimidated by politicians whose decisions are moving us rapidly towards global destruction and bloodshed.

Everything is interrelated. Among indigenous peoples, this idea is readily acknowledged but rarely is the subtle implication of this truism appreciated. If we return to the visions of our elders, acknowledge the interrelatedness of people, the Earth and the Sacred, and accept the interdependence of all facets of our societies, we find our place in the broader whole. This "grounding" provides us with the strength and fortitude to persist in the face of sometimes overwhelming odds.

The history of the indigenous peoples whose lands America occupies demonstrates that the United States has sought to circumvent self-determination by replacing indigenous governmental structures with Western political systems. This was accomplished through legislative and statutory measures (such as the Indian Reorganization Act and the State of Hawaii Sovereignty Elections Committee). In some instances, the United States has pursued administrative policies of nonrecognition and the termination of indigenous governments in order to seize control over their lands and natural resources for development and militarism.

The United States has been able to accomplish this subversion with the cooperation of natives who have assimilated or who have been able to obtain power and wealth for themselves. If we are to change the course of our future and regain our rightful place in our traditional lands, we must struggle to attain positions of leadership in our own native governments and advocate for justice at the highest levels in the national and international arenas.

Merging the Traditional and the Modern

Because of colonization, there are few indigenous cultures that can live as our elders did in traditional times. Modern development and political systems have impacted our lives and forever changed the way in which we communicate and address social and environmental issues. Modern technology, systems, and practices can be utilized by indigenous peoples to meet their current needs; but such applications should be "culturally appropriate," which means that they need to conform to traditional values and support traditional cultural undertakings.

We will make a critical error if we, as indigenous peoples, only support "traditional technologies." In today's world, we must acquire new skills and find new solutions to our modern problems.

In traditional times, our ceremonial practices and social systems were sufficient to maintain balance and to support our cultures. This is no longer true in many instances. Native peoples today need to understand environmental toxicity and degradation and to develop programs for natural resource management that employ soil and water testing techniques and other scientific methods. In addressing the social and psychological needs of our peoples, we must be able to understand fetal alcohol syndrome, AIDS, and drug addiction and to develop clinical programs that are "culturally appropriate."

In any case, the initial inquiry is not whether modern methods, devices, or technologies should be used, but which of these methods is most culturally appropriate for our peoples. In this context, the motto of the Indigenous Women's Network is most instructive:

"Let us, as indigenous women, strive to nurture and sustain our cultures and communities, to alleviate poverty, to achieve self-sufficiency and to achieve these goals by keeping within the visions of our elders, applying culturally appropriate technology and sustaining our spirits through the practice of our religious traditions."

By applying this motto to our daily lives, we will bring about peaceful change in our local and international communities. There is much that needs to be done, but our capacity to achieve our goals is unquestionable.

Notes

This speech was delivered in September 1994 at a metting of the Indigenous Women's Network.

1. In 1993, the United Nations sponsored a global consultation on human rights in Vienna, Austria. This was the first such consultation in over twenty years. Its focus was on human rights violations globally.

15

A Transformational Feminism

GERDA LERNER

———•◆•———

Gerda Lerner, Ph.D., is professor emerita at the University of Wisconsin, Madison. The first woman in fifty years to be elected president of the Organization of American Historians (1981–1982), she has received numerous honors, including the American Historical Association's Award for Scholarly Distinction (1992). She is the author of numerous books, among them *The Female Experience: An American Documentary; Women and History: The Creation of Patriarchy, Vol. I; Women and History: The Creation of Feminist Consciousness,* *from the Middle Ages to 1870 A.D., Vol. II; Black Women in White America: A Documentary History;* and a collection of essays, *Why History Matters* (1997).

———•◆•———

woman of power: What directions would you like to see feminists take in this decade in order to facilitate leadership within local and international movements?

Gerda Lerner: First of all, I want to say that I consider feminism a practical, political program for the transformation of society, one that holds solutions for women and men. I consider it the most promising of the social programs now in existence. It is a practical, transformational program, philosophy, and political agenda. I believe that in order for the world to survive the twenty-first century with all the dangers that are now present—namely, nuclear power, rampant militarism, ecological dangers, and what I consider a ticking time bomb: the maldistribution of resources in the world—we must adopt feminist solutions to these problems.

And why feminism? Well, first of all, because the system of patriarchy which was built in the Bronze Age, in approximately the first millennium B.C. in Western civilization, arose out of a combination of militarism and the agricultural revolution. It created a system of hierarchical government, dominated by militarism, in which men hold the resources and distribute them to women who are either members of their family of birth or linked to them through a sexual relationship; they also share resources with subordinate men. As long as patriarchy exists, despite other changes we make in society—for example, efforts to fight racism, militarism, hatred of various minority groups—patriarchy will always reconstitute itself and create other hierarchical systems. The emancipation of women is essential to ending these hierarchical systems.

That's one reason. The second one is that because women are half the population and are represented in every group of the population, in every class, in every region, they cannot be put down like other groups have been. Other groups that have asked for transformational change or for revolutionary change have been defeated and wiped out. You cannot defeat half the human race. Therefore, women are the main instrument for making change.

Third, I believe that in the twenty-first century, violent overthrow and revolutions will no longer be possible. They only lead to increased violence and a cycle of violence, as we have seen in various places in the world today. So, instead of violent overthrow, there has to be a peaceful transition and transformation of society, and women are ideally located and ideally situated to lead that kind of movement.

And fourth, all of this can be accomplished only if feminism and women's leadership are used to build large coalitions with other movements such as the ecology movement, the movement for racial justice, movements against various other oppressive systems like anti-Semitism

and ethnic hatred, and movements for a more just redistribution of resources, or economic justice. If we learn to build these coalitions, we can
really transform society.

*woman of power: Are there any changes that you would like to see the feminist
movement make?*

Lerner: I would like to see the feminist movement be much more concerned with the most oppressed groups in society. So, I would like to see
as a firmly established priority our defense of poor women, of women on
welfare, of women who are without health insurance, and of children
(who are today one of the most oppressed groups in society). I would like
to see that goal be central to our activities rather than the promotion of
the emancipation of middle-class women only. I am not saying that we
have done only that, but I think that there has been a great deal of emphasis on the emancipation of middle-class women and that we have ne-
glected the women that need help the most, so I would like to see the feminist movement make those issues central to its agenda in every area.

I would also like to see us conduct the fight against racism, sexism, na-
tionalism, and anti-Semitism as if they were *connected* rather than separate issues. There is no way that we can abolish any of these evils unless
we abolish them all. And unless we learn how to combine these issues,
we are going to get nowhere. We are going to take one step forward, and
six steps backwards, as we have until now.

*woman of power: Are there other specific issues for which you would like to see
feminists provide leadership?*

Lerner: Yes, for example, very specifically right now with so-called welfare reform in the forefront of the political debate over the spectrum of society from reactionary Republicans to liberal Democrats, I would like the
women's movement to resist this formulation of the issue. I would like to
see us expose the phony nature of this attack and insist upon addressing
the causes of the poverty and abuse now being experienced by poor people. As long as we treat as separate political issues the different forms in
which hierarchy keeps the various groups subordinated, we attack symptoms rather than root causes. Hierarchical systems need various target
groups that they can define as deviant. At the moment, Black teenage
mothers have been demonized as "welfare queens." We must show the
linkage of their situation with that of white women on welfare and with

that of the working poor, female and male, in order to show that the tactics of dividing victims from one another will not work. If we do not learn that by doing that we are defending ourselves, then I have very little hope that we are going to be able to make a valid social movement out of feminism in the twenty-first century.

What we have to keep in mind all the time is that we are not a movement of an "interest group," we are not a movement of a "minority," we are a movement embracing half the human race, half the nation. We have to act that way.

woman of power: How do you think women can best support the leadership of activists and visionaries in the feminist movement?

Lerner: Well, first of all, I feel that the women's movement has not sufficiently used women's history as a tool for organizing. Our journals and our publications have paid very little attention to women's history. We have not analyzed the strategies and tactics of the women who came before us, nor have we fully understood their ideas so that we learn from them and do not have to repeat what they have already done. And so, in every women's organization, I would like to see specific attention paid to the goal of bringing in women's history as a tool for consciousness raising, as a tool for learning, as a tool for giving perspective to women in their struggles.

One highly effective tool for raising community awareness on feminist issues has been the celebration of Women's History Month. The National Women's History Network has developed teaching tools, such as posters, games, and various instructional materials, for schools at all levels. In many communities, libraries, schools, and various organizations have worked together to celebrate women's achievements and leadership during Women's History Month. Another way that local organizations can use women's history is to use older women as resources. Meetings in which older women, representing various ethnic and racial groups in society share their life experiences and talk about the organizational work they did in the past can be inspiring and educational for younger women.

woman of power: Is there considerable overlap with previous historical movements?

Lerner: Well, what I see is that we have not learned from history. For example, the nineteenth century women's movement built the largest coalition in American history around the issue of suffrage. We deal with it always as if we need to learn who were the true leaders, the high points, and so on, but there are many other lessons to be learned—about how you build such a coalition, and what happens to the various parts of the coalition, and how you can advance over the position that they had.

For example, Florence Kelley (1859–1932), general secretary of the National Consumers League, mobilized consumers to ensure that goods were manufactured under decent working conditions. Sixty Consumer Leagues in twenty states, which she organized, boycotted goods made under sweatshop conditions. Her vision, to make use of middle-class women's power as consumers to help working-class women, created a powerful instrument of pressure for the passage of legislation regarding wages and hours and for an end to child labor. Incidentally, it also created an important feminist coalition that endured for several decades.

We desperately need such a movement today. Most people are totally unaware of it; they have no idea that this has been done before. There are many such examples.

If you look at the history of reform, over the entire span of American history, you will see that in every reform movement in American history, the record of white women working with women of color has been better than the record of white men working with men of color. It hasn't been perfect, and it hasn't been as good as it should be, but it has been better. There are things we could learn from that: How was it done? What was done wrong? And so on. I think that is a very important issue.

woman of power: How else do you think we can support women leaders?

Lerner: I think you are putting too much emphasis on leadership. Our job is to build grassroots struggle. Our job is to create leaders out of people who are not leaders according to the media definition of a leader, and to honor them, and to learn from them, and to allow them to go on with their lives in positions where they may have only local leadership. That was the strength of the old women's movement. That was the way women have always worked. We have worked locally to affect national issues. Today, if there were less emphasis on leadership and more emphasis on grassroots organizing, I think we would get further.

A good example of how this has been done successfully has been in the struggle against violence against women, where feminists have organized locally in various forms. You hardly know the name of a single woman who has done this kind of work, but it has been a grassroots movement with tremendous impact on society as a whole. If we could transfer that kind of model to other political issues, paying less attention to advancing the careers of leaders than we do to building the grassroots organization that sustains leaders, we would be better off.

woman of power: You may have already addressed this issue in part, in the sense that you think "leadership" needs to be redefined; what, if any, obstacles to women's leadership are of concern to you?

Lerner: A "leader" in America in the twentieth century generally means somebody who makes a career out of the concerns, and issues, and political demands of other people; and who, as soon as she or he has attained a so-called position of leadership, is then a public figure who becomes corrupted to the point of no longer really leading anybody but her or himself and the media. Now, not everybody does that. Gloria Steinem, at the beginning of the women's movement, coined a phrase and practice that she herself has practiced, but very few other women have, and that is: "Wherever you go, take another woman with you." That is leadership. But leadership is not a matter of being known, and being famous, and being interviewed, and being on TV programs, and being written up in the newspapers.

My concept of leadership is embodied by somebody like Ella Baker (1903–1986), who was the foremost organizer of the civil rights movement, yet, until recently, hardly anybody knew her name. Leader of the NAACP in the 1940s, executive secretary of the Southern Christian Leadership Conference (SCLC) in the 1950s, founder and chief source of inspiration for the Student Nonviolent Coordinating Committee (SNCC) in the 1960s, this African-American woman was the guiding spirit and the organizing genius behind the civil rights movement. A leader of similar caliber was Katherine Clarenbach (1921–1994) who, as chairperson of the National Committees on the Status of Women, was one of the founders of NOW and its first organizer. Later, as organizer of the First National Women's Conference in Houston, Texas, in 1977, she was at the center of the greatest network of women's organizations ever created. Like Ella Baker, she shunned publicity, but her leadership was inspiring and lasting. We need to model our ideal of leadership after women such as these.

To me, the woman who creates a local organization that continues to function after she is gone is exercising leadership. Leadership is creating something that lives on without you.

woman of power: So, when you define what you consider to be the essential facets of leadership, one of them would be to create something that lives beyond you?

Lerner: Absolutely, to create something that replaces and surpasses you, that has a life of its own because there are many people who will be drawn into it and who will give leadership to it as a group, even if you move on or go away. To me, that has always been the measure of leadership. If you can do that, you're a leader. If you can't do that, you're just a media personality.

woman of power: How have variables such as gender, ethnicity, religion, social class, and so on, shaped your ideas about your leadership role?

Lerner: I never thought about leadership. I still don't think about leadership. I think about a goal that I want to achieve. I wanted, for example, to make women's history an accepted part of every academic curriculum from elementary school to the Ph.D.—that was my goal. I didn't give any thought to leadership. I thought about how that could be done. In other words, I analyzed where you would have to start, and what you would have to do, and then I tried to take whatever measures I could to interest other people—the main thing is to enlist other people to work on that goal with you. The point is that wherever we are as women, wherever we are situated in our lives, we can advance a feminist agenda if we stop thinking about how to be leaders and think rather about how to be doers, how to be agents.

How have race, gender, and so on affected me? Well, I'm a woman, right? And I'm a Jew, and I have suffered persecution at the hand of the Nazis. I have, therefore, understood very early that you can't win any kind of rights and freedoms if you tolerate measures for dividing people, such as racism and anti-Semitism. If you allow these systems to exist and do not resist them, then you can't attain any kind of emancipation. So that is something that I learned in my own life, and I have always tried to illustrate that to other people. When I came to America, I became very interested in the situation of people of color, because they are the primary victims of racism here in this country, whereas in Europe, Jews were the primary victims of racism. Because I understood that, I was interested from the start in struggling against racism and in linking the two issues.

If everybody goes just one or two steps forward, we can change the world. But if you are concerned about how to be a leader, all you are really concerned about is how you can fit into the patriarchal system in order to receive rewards, and that is not the way to go. That is not our problem. Our problem is to redefine organizational leadership, to figure out what it means and how to sustain it over a long period of time. The thing that hurts me the most is when I hear women saying "Well, we've struggled so hard, and now feminism is in retreat and there's a backlash and I'm discouraged"—after only four or five years. That's ridiculous.

It took seventy-two years of unremitting organization and struggle for women to secure the rights of suffrage. It took over one hundred years to eliminate child labor. It took over one hundred and thirty years of organizing and political agitation for workers to win the right to unionize and to bargain collectively.

Another modern example of a successful coalition is the antilynching movement. It was begun in the 1890s by the African-American journalist and club woman Ida Wells-Barnett and carried forward by the Black women's club movement. It was not until 1920 that white club women hesitantly engaged in some joint efforts with Black women to stop lynchings. They did not succeed until the 1930s when the Association of Southern Women for Prevention of Lynching (ASWPL) was organized. The tenuous and often conflict-ridden cooperation of Black and white women finally, in the 1940s, changed public opinion nationwide without ever succeeding in Congress passing an antilynching bill.

As history teaches us, any movement that cannot be sustained for fifty or a hundred years is not likely to accomplish its goal. For the future of feminism, we need grassroots organization. We need a long-range perspective. We need people with staying power.

16

Beyond Critique and Vision–Global Leadership in the Twenty-First Century

CHARLOTTE BUNCH

———•◆•———

Charlotte Bunch, feminist author and organizer for over twenty-five years, was a founder of the early feminist group Washington D.C. Women's Liberation and of *Quest: A Feminist Quarterly.* Editor of seven anthologies, her latest books are *Passionate Politics: Feminist Theory in Action* and *Demanding Accountability: The Global Campaign and Vienna Tribunal for Women's Human Rights.*

Now director of the Douglass College Center for Women's Global Leadership and professor in the Bloustein School of Planning and Public Policy at Rutgers University, Bunch has been working on issues of global feminism with organizations around the world since the 1980s.

The Center for Women's Global Leadership works to enhance the leadership of women on global issues and was responsible for coordinating the Global Campaign for Women's Human Rights at the 1993 U.N. World

Conference on Human Rights in Vienna, Austria. The Center also coordi-
nated the women's human rights caucus and other activities for the U.N.
Fourth World Conference on Women held in Beijing, China, in 1995.

*woman of power: How would you describe the goals of the Center for Women's
Global Leadership?*

Charlotte Bunch: We started the Center out of an interest in what was
happening to women internationally. We knew that although there was a
lot of women's leadership taking place at the grassroots level, women
were terribly underrepresented in the more structured public-policy
arena, not only at the elective level but also at the administrative level in
the major nongovernmental and governmental bodies that feed into the
making of public policy.

We wanted to build a greater consciousness of gender in that world.
The main work of the Center has been to bring together women who are
activist leaders at the grassroots level in different parts of the world (including the United States, but not primarily) to strategize, and to introduce them to the ways in which they can have an impact on public policy.
We have chosen to do that with issues of violence against women and human rights as a focus. The other part of it has been to provide a gender
perspective on the issues that are being discussed in the public policy
world.

We work with women leaders in leadership training, developing, and
building strategies and networks around the issues of women and human
rights. We also engage in gender analysis of these issues and try to move
into some of the mainstream human-rights organizations, as well as some
of the United Nations agencies, to show them what it means to take gender into account, and how gender is a factor in policies related to human
rights, peace, development, and so on.

That is what you could call the concept of the Center, and we put it into
action through an annual Leadership Institute, an international campaign
on violence against women as a human rights issue, and through the
work we have been doing for the various U.N. world conferences.

*woman of power: How do you select participants for the annual Leadership
Institute?*

Bunch: These women are activists from grassroots organizations around
the world. We send out an application form every year to several thou-

sand women's organizations and networks. We receive and screen about two hundred applications and then accept around twenty to twenty-five women, fairly evenly distributed throughout the world. We look for women who have accomplished some organizational activist leadership at the local level but who have not necessarily had an opportunity to apply that work internationally.

woman of power: Does the Center have ongoing projects throughout the year?

Bunch: Our major program focus is on the annual Leadership Institute, but we also have smaller, strategic planning activities. The other program focus is the annual international campaign called the Sixteen Days of Activism against Gender Violence, which was created as a public campaign to bring attention to violence against women at a public-policy level and to show in particular the relationship between violence against women and human rights, which has been the centerpiece of our gender perspective on human rights work.

Part of our strategy is the idea that leadership for social action does not happen in a vacuum, so leadership training is not done in the abstract. I think each of us develops our leadership skills because we care about making something happen; therefore, any training that we do has to be connected to some common goal, and we have chosen women's human rights. Initially, we chose the issue of violence against women because we felt that it best illustrated what the absence of a gender consciousness had led to: a worldwide, human rights movement that had never considered violence against women as a human rights issue.

woman of power: What kind of work is the Center doing with the United Nations on the Universal Declaration of Human Rights and the agenda for the Fourth World Conference on Women?

Bunch: When we first began to look for ways to make visible what women were thinking on the international scale in 1990, we realized that the U.N. world conferences were useful arenas where women had been heard. The women's conferences throughout the U.N. Decade for Women, which began in Mexico City, Mexico, in 1975, and continued in 1980 in Copenhagen, Denmark, and ended in 1985 in Nairobi, Kenya, have been among the few arenas where women have had the opportunity to move beyond their own country's work and to conceive of themselves as an international movement. The next conference in that series, the U.N. Fourth World Conference on Women, will be held in Beijing, China, in September of 1995.

Those conferences also taught a lot of us, myself included, that the United Nations is a very powerful location for international public debate. This is not to say that the United Nations actually controls policies, but a lot of the discussion about policy and what people need now takes place there. Those of us who had been active in the women's conferences began to realize that women needed to be present at other U.N. conferences too, and in all the different agencies, not simply in the separate women's activities, which are, of course, marginal to most of the public policy work.

Over the past five or six years, different groups have taken up that issue: for example, women got very involved in organizing around the U.N. Conference on Environment and Development in Rio de Janeiro, Brazil, in 1992 and the International Conference on Population and Development in Cairo, Egypt, in 1994. Our Center organized women for the World Conference on Human Rights, held in Vienna, Austria, in 1993, where our goal was to make visible specific ways that women's human rights are violated that are not always identical to the ways in which men's are. Many of us are now looking at this next conference in Beijing as an occasion when women can talk about affecting the political world in terms of a whole spectrum of issues: environment, human rights, development, peace, and population.

woman of power: How do you think feminism can meet the critical need for moral leadership in local, national, and world politics?

Bunch: The world desperately needs the new kinds of thinking that women can provide. I don't think that women are any more pure or moral than men, but since women have not been imbedded in the power structures, they may be able to provide some original thinking about strategies that are not so tied to the systems of domination. We can perhaps shake up some of the established dominations and bring in a more justice-oriented vision of public policy at a local, national, and international level.

woman of power: Are there specific changes that you would like to see the feminist movement make globally in order to foster women's leadership?

Bunch: We have gained a healthy ability to criticize and a healthy degree of scepticism about male leadership, authoritarian power, and domination, but we haven't yet learned how to create positive models of leadership. You can't only be a critic of the world. You also have to try to find positive models for changing it, and that includes models for leadership and for affecting public policy. That is much more difficult than merely criticizing what's wrong with someone else's way of doing things. We have tended not to be very supportive of our own leaders and we, therefore, have had a difficult time moving from critique to the creation of actual alternatives.

I think one of the challenges that the various women's movements (the various manifestations of feminism) face, and one of the crucial challenges in this next decade, will be to translate critique and vision into real alternatives in public policy, finding forms of leadership that we can support so that we can move forward.

woman of power: Do you find that leadership programs like yours enhance this kind of perspective in a way that isn't possible at a grassroots level?

Bunch: Institutes like ours give leaders an opportunity to see themselves in a broader context and to share their experiences with women in other parts of the world: for example, one of the most common problems is that after a certain point, there is not a lot of support for leadership in local groups. There is a lot of fear about women moving into public policy-making positions and being seen by the outside world as representing other women.

At an institute like ours, women leaders feel less isolated. They start to recognize how their problems are similar, if not identical, to the problems of women in other countries. They stop feeling that it is their fault. Many women think, for example, "Oh, it's just something in my country," and they start to see that this is a broader problem. Therefore, they feel less immobilized and start to exchange solutions. An institute like ours is a drop in the bucket, but every woman who comes here must have a commitment to take these ideas back to a larger group of people, to expand the discussion.

woman of power: You have said elsewhere that "Lesbians' ideas on leadership or poverty need to be present along with our views on sexuality and homophobia."[1] Would you elaborate on that idea?

Bunch: I think that I was referring to the idea that lesbians, like women of color and any other group with an identity politics, have at least two types of leadership. One is the leadership you take around that particular identity issue, in which you present the lesbian rights aspects of an issue. For example, within the human rights movement, there are certain questions that need to be raised, such as: How are lesbian rights also human rights?

That is one form of lesbian leadership, but the other form, which is what has more often been denied, is the ways in which lesbians and others also have a lot to say about *any* issue. To me, it is the same thing we are saying now about women, that we don't only have things to say about "women's issues." You have asked specific questions about lesbian leadership and women of color leadership, but more and more, I am interested in the women's movement supporting all women's ability to speak on whatever range of issues they care about.

woman of power: Do you mean that because we have had identity politics for a certain number of years, it is now possible for us to move on to talk about leadership in a different way?

Bunch: I think it is possible, but I do not think it is going to be easy. From my point of view as an activist, however, I think it is absolutely necessary. Otherwise, no one can speak about anything except her own particular experience. The real challenge is to make sure that each one of us takes into account as many different voices as possible.

The challenge for me, as I see it, is to incorporate as many different experiences of women as possible into my own analysis or vision: to be inclusive in what I say, and to open as much space as possible for other women to be heard, too. But if I think that I can't say anything because I don't have enough authentic experience on certain issues, then I end up further silencing those issues. If I am afraid, for example, as a white woman, to say anything about racism because I'll be speaking about "somebody else's" issues, then I perpetuate silence about racism. But these issues affect all of us. They are not somebody else's issues. You have to take risks, put forth your own vision, and learn through criticism, but not be afraid to speak.

I think identity politics has the danger of silencing people rather than giving voice to more people, and of separating people to the point where we forget that the reason for identity politics is so that no one dominant view is allowed to overtake others. The good thing about identity politics is that it recognizes that those with dominant power have tended to speak for others without taking their views into account—that they have subsumed the others—and now that we know that, the struggle is not to do that anymore.

woman of power: So, in other words, with the issues of nondominant groups always being placed at the center and fully acknowledged, we can begin to talk about other issues?

Bunch: On any issue—human rights is a good example because it is a very broad issue—you try to ensure that the voices of nondominant groups are heard so that there isn't one universalizing tendency. But we do want to try to define some common points of reference. For example, in working on the issue of violence against women, we do not assume that there is one form of violence that everybody has in common or makes an equal priority, but we do assume that women in all cultures see violence as something they want to eliminate. The goal is to do something about it, not just to have the voices heard.

Some of the discussion of these issues sounds almost as if the goal were to attain the perfect statement of the issue, but the goal is *change.* You need to have as much clarity as possible, but if you get so involved in making sure you have the perfect statement or in preserving the purity of your group, you are not able to do anything in the world.

woman of power: How do you think women can best support the leadership of activists and visionaries in the feminist, spiritual, and political movements?

Bunch: I think the best support we could give to each other would be, first of all, to start treating each other with respect and, where we disagree, to assume that everyone is doing what they do out of the best possible motive. The point is to assume that we are doing this because we want to make change and not because we are all out to get power. If we did that, we could create a movement where women leaders were respected for what they are trying to do.

What disturbs me the most in some parts of the women's movement is the lack of respect for each other. I have no problem with critique, but I do object to its being made in an accusatory, disrespectful way.

woman of power: Can you suggest any specific strategies to achieve respectful critique?

Bunch: The greatest strategy I know of is to talk honestly to each other and to ask ourselves whether there is an ethics in the feminist movement about how we treat one another. The question I keep raising is: What do we hope to achieve in the world, and how do our interactions with each other build toward that goal?

It helps to remember why we are doing this work. I think there is sometimes the naive assumption that if we talk about it enough, we will get it perfect, and I don't believe in perfection. I don't believe the world will ever be perfect, or that any of us will ever be perfect, or that our strategies will ever be perfect. In the effort to make social change, we learn and grow and develop, and that is what it is all about.

woman of power: What do you envision as the role of women's spiritual leaders in the 1990s and beyond?

Bunch: My sense of the spiritual is as an aspect of being human, and you can't leave out the spiritual dimension in a comprehensive movement for change. My problem with spirituality, as with so much else in this culture, is that it tends to be seen as totally separate from the political or economic dimensions, by both the spiritual and the political movements. Some of the women's spirituality leaders lose sight of the political/economic arena, and that bothers me because spirituality has to be connected to where we are moving politically as well.

Because it is a more personal dimension, it is hard to talk about what spirituality means in our movement politically, but it is important not to lose sight of it because we have seen how the various right-wing religious forces are able to manipulate people's spiritual needs because the feminist and progressive movements have not spoken adequately to that dimension.

woman of power: How do you think your background has empowered you to do the kind of work that you have chosen to do?

Bunch: My mother was very active in civic and community affairs in the small town in New Mexico where we lived. So, I grew up with a role model in that she considered the issues raised in the public arena of our town relevant to her life. Both of my parents gave me the feeling that my opinions about the world mattered. At least on the level of conversation, there was no distinction made between girls and boys in our family, and I think that was very important.

Another piece of my background that exposed me to the idea of women in public affairs was my experience at Duke University in North Carolina in the early sixties, at the beginning of the civil rights movement. My relationship to that movement was through the women's college at Duke which reinforced women's leadership in many ways and provided a training ground because we took leadership in our own student organizations.

At Duke, I was involved in sit-ins and support work in the progressive churches where both black and white women served as strong role models for me. After college, I moved to Washington, D.C., where I focused on community organizing, and the antiracism and later the antiimperial-ist/antiwar part of the 1960s movement. When I began to work at the Institute for Policy Studies, a left-oriented think tank, for the first time, I encountered resistance to women as leaders. I think I became a feminist in part because I had experienced fairly strong acceptance for women's leadership in local, community level work until I reached that level of policy making. I had the expectation that I had something to offer, but it was much more of a 1960s definition of leadership: the notion that we were all in this together, and that there were things one could do to make change.

After that, I became very involved in the first women's liberation group in Washington, D.C., initially called the Radical Women's Discussion Group and then Washington D.C. Women's Liberation; various collectives, such as the Daughters of Lilith; and then I came out as a lesbian and we started the Furies Collective, so I moved into lesbian feminist politics.

woman of power: *In view of your own positive experiences as a child, do you have any ideas about how leadership skills might be fostered in young women and girls?*

Bunch: I believe that it is very important for girls to have girls-only organizations because, as feminist research has shown, in environments where there are no boys, girls do assert their leadership. But if you put girls into mixed environments only, especially in their early years, the social preference for male leaders greatly impedes girls' development.

I think it is very important to have community organizations where girls initiate activities such as campaigns to collect clothing for victims of a hurricane; activities that engage them with the experience of what I call "the public world." But clubs of this kind must have some connection to what people internationally call "civil society," the structure of society around you.

If I had to pick my emphasis, I would start with really encouraging girls' leadership in spaces for girls only. For example, although the U.S. Congress is not my view of the only arena for leadership, it's an easy one to measure, and it has been found that a very high percentage of the women in Congress went to women's colleges.

Girls with leadership potential also need to be given encouragement. That is not a matter of encouraging them to see themselves as isolated, separate individuals, or of tracking them ahead of other girls. Rather, it is to encourage the kind of leadership that, in some ways, women have been the best at: leadership that involves you with other people in making things happen. Women do that all the time, but it is not often given outlet into the public world.

woman of power: What do you consider some of the essential facets of good leadership?

Bunch: Let me take that question in two parts. I want to take off the word "good," and talk, first, about leadership and, second, about the ethics and values that we apply to leadership. If leadership began to be understood as simply one of many traits one can have, we would be better off.

Perhaps one of the most important elements of leadership in the public sphere is having some kind of vision and then articulating that vision. So, leadership involves both conceptualization and articulation: seeing what needs to happen, and then knowing how to bring people together in order to meet some particular political goal or community need. This involves an understanding of both people and processes. Many women, for example, can analyze intellectually what ought to happen, but they don't have the ability to mobilize or inspire others to do it. And some women are charismatic, but they don't really have the analytical ability to illustrate how to make things happen; and women who are good at envisioning how to move out into new territory may not be very good at organizational leadership, the daily maintenance of the structures that keep an institution going.

One of our problems is that we usually expect a leader to do everything well. Some women *do* have a particularly good combination of these skills but, by and large, most women are better at one or another. If you have a leadership team, women with various skills can work together. So, leaders can have different pieces of these skills, but they certainly have to have some combination of them if they are to be effective.

Now, if those are the skills of leadership, what makes it "good" or "bad" leadership, if you will, is the political and ethical commitments that you bring to that activity. I don't think that any one person is inherently a good or a bad leader (and I am here speaking of "good" and "bad" in the moral sense)—their principles determine that. Here is where the feminist questions about leadership become so important. I would like to add that when I speak about "women," I mean the gender that has been constructed by the social order (if it's biological, we don't know it, and I don't necessarily even consider it the relevant question anymore). I do assume, however, that women have developed more tendencies toward a cooperative, consensus-building style of leadership because in order to survive in families, which have been our primary arena, women have had to foster consensus and cooperation. I think that is one of the things we know how to do better, and it is very useful in leadership.

However, consensus and cooperation can also be a trap, because there are moments when you may have to do something in spite of not having consensus, and men have often been better at that than women, so we need to learn a balance of these skills. The male model of leadership, on the other hand, has been of this lone figure who pioneers the path, and that's nonsense too. No one can lead that way, because a leader must have followers.

woman of power: *How can we overcome what you have called "the dynamic of domination" in our efforts to support the leadership of other women and to take responsible leadership ourselves?*

Bunch: This dynamic of dualism and domination of one group by another as the only mode of accommodating difference is something that is deeply rooted and insidious—this win/lose dichotomy that results in male/female, white/Black, and so on. You have to eradicate it on the political and the personal level at the same time, and it is a slow process. I think that there has been considerable progress on the personal level, especially among feminists, and who knows how that will affect the political arena as it moves out into the discourse?

woman of power: *You have lived through several of the women's movement experiments with leadership. What is your perspective on those ideas now, and how have your ideas about leadership evolved as a result?*

Bunch: In the early days of the feminist movement in the United States, there was a tendency to deny leadership, to see all leadership as somehow patriarchal and authoritarian, and to overemphasize the collective experience of women. In many ways, it was perhaps a necessary corrective to our society's overconcentration on authoritarian models. But in other ways, it was destructive as well.

If you look at the movement as a whole, and I look at movements from an historical point of view, all of these trends had their usefulness as a way of expressing the need for new thinking about leadership, and that was good. On the other hand, on the individual level, it was often disastrous because women who had leadership skills were not allowed to operate openly. If you wanted to make something happen, for example, you had to pretend that you weren't making it happen, that it was just the will of the group. That created even more unaccountable leadership because if leaders (in most organizations there are usually two or three people who play clear leadership roles) are not acknowledged, neither can they be held accountable.

We are no longer a single movement, and those early experiments showed us that we want responsible leadership that doesn't see itself as separate from the group. We want leadership that tries to reflect what is going on in that group but also lends it direction and coherence. We no longer assume "Anybody could do that," and I think we've learned that you can't exercise leadership if you only reflect your group's opinion. A leader needs to be able to move ahead a little bit and see what is coming.

woman of power: What direction would you like to see feminists take in this decade in order to facilitate leadership within local, national, and global movements?

Bunch: I think we have gone beyond the phase of just looking at our own issues, not that we are finished with that entirely. We have learned a lot from our local movements that can be applied to global issues and I would like to see that happen. Other women may not agree, but I think that it is time to move women's issues to the center of the mainstream public discourse, in the sense that bell hooks talks about moving from margin to center, so that issues such as violence, and economic development, and injustice are seen from within a woman's perspective, so that that perspective is integral to thinking about every issue.

———————•◆•———————

The Center for Women's Global Leadership

The Center for Women's Global Leadership was founded as a project of Douglass College in 1989 and is a component of the Rutgers Institute for Women's Leadership. The Center seeks to develop an understanding of the ways in which gender affects the exercise of power and the conduct of public policy internationally. The Center's activities consider women's leadership and transformative visions as crucial to every policy area from democratization and human rights, to global security and economic restructuring. The Center also works to give visibility to abuses of women's human rights by challenging the current understanding and implementation of international human rights policy and processes. In collaboration with women's groups around the world, the Center endeavors to hold governments and the international human rights community accountable for the promotion and protection of women's human rights.

The Center's activities include:

Leadership Institutes

Each year, the Center holds a two-week intensive residential Women's Global Leadership Institute. Designed for women leaders at the grassroots and national levels, the Institutes provide opportunities for women to exchange experiences and develop global responses to violations of women's human rights. In addition, the Center cosponsors and participates in regional workshops and institutes with similar goals.

Strategic Planning Activities

The Center sponsors programs that bring women together to plan and coordinate specific strategies around women's human rights globally. These have included an ongoing Working Group on Women and Human Rights comprised of activists, academics, and professionals; a Strategic Planning Institute prior to the U.N. World Conference on Human Rights; a Strategic Planning Institute exploring women's human rights in the U.S.; and with the U.N. Division for the Advancement of Women, an Expert Group Meeting on eradicating violence against women. Strategic planning activities also target other U.N. forums such as the Fourth World Conference on Women in September, 1995.

International Mobilization Campaigns

The Center has played a leading role in organizing international mobilization campaigns as part of the Global Campaign for Women's Human Rights. Among these campaigns are:

- **Sixteen Days of Activism Against Gender Violence**—The Center coordinates an annual global campaign that highlights gender-based violence as a human rights issue and links hundreds of groups organizing locally.
- **Global Petition Campaign**—The Center facilitates an ongoing collection of signatures calling upon the U.N. to promote and protect the human rights of women. In June 1993, a half million signatures gathered by women in one hundred and twenty-four countries were presented to the World Conference on Human Rights in Vienna. A new petition calls upon the U.N. to report to the World Women's Conference on its implementation of the Vienna Declaration's commitment to women's human rights.
- **Global Tribunals and Hearings on Women's Human Rights**—The Center organizes and encourages hearings to document violations of women's hu-

man rights. At the World Conference on Human Rights, the Vienna Tribunal featured women from twenty-five countries who testified to violations of women's human rights perpetrated by both state and private actors in socioeconomic, political, and cultural contexts.

Global Education

The Center frequently conducts forums on women's human rights at a wide variety of conferences and sponsors regular global education gatherings in the New Jersey/New York area featuring international and local speakers. The Center also works to introduce women's global perspectives into Rutgers University. A small resource library contains publications from women's organizations globally and other information pertinent to the Center's work. The Center also responds to specific crises affecting women around the world through letter-writing campaigns and other actions. Visiting associates and student interns at the Center pursue their own research and contribute to its programs.

Notes

1. "Diversity and Feminism," unpublished working paper presented at the Laurie Chair Seminar, "Feminist Perspectives on Leadership, Power, and Diversity," Rutgers University, 1989.

Women's Global Leadership Institute, 1992

About the Book
and Editor

This collection brings together a number of key interviews with some of the most interesting, visionary, and thought-provoking feminist theorists and activists now working in the United States. It provides a detailed exploration into their responses to feminist paradigm shifts, their analyses of the future of the women's movement, and their globally constructed theories for transformational change with an emphasis on positive social change, empowerment, and compassionate action. Illustrating how the women's movement has begun to create the language and the critical mass necessary to effect vital spiritual, cultural, and social transformation, the book offers a fascinating look at how women are moving beyond dichotomizations of culture, resisting or refusing the bifurcations between theory and practice, politics and spirituality. This collection provides cross-cultural and historicized examples of how this integration has been and continues to be realized by women and others who are seeking to transform their societies.

This collection will serve as an excellent source of contemporary material for courses exploring the confluence of the many branches of feminism, or "feminisms," reflecting the women's movement's existing diversity and continued growth as a movement for positive social change.

Gail Hanlon, a poet and writer, was associate editor of *woman of power* magazine from 1991 to 1995.

Photo Credits

Nancy Reiko Kato, courtesy of Kathleen Merrigan, *Freedom Socialist*
Andrea Dworkin, courtesy of Arne Svenson
Deborah Anna Luepnitz, courtesy of Deborah Lamb
Karen Brodkin Sacks, courtesy of Sharon Bays
Riane Eisler, courtesy of David Loye
Gerda Lerner, courtesy of Martina Thierkopf
Charlotte Bunch, courtesy of Terry Lorant
Women's Global Leadership Institute 1992, courtesy of Boni Luna